ON
HUMAN SLAUGHTER

Evil, Justice, Mercy

ELIZABETH BRUENIG

zando

NEW YORK

CONTENTS

Introduction   vii

A Good Man, at One Time   1

Can America Kill Its Prisoners Kindly?   19

Two Executions on a Thursday in America   31

Should the Parkland Shooter Die?   38

Dead to Rights   44

Dead Man Living   61

Death of a Sinner   79

On Murders Especially Heinous, Atrocious, or Cruel   87

A History of Violence   92

Alabama Makes Plans to Gas Its Prisoners   111

Article Credits   121

About the Author   123

INTRODUCTION

_____

I HAD THOUGHT MORE ABOUT my immortality than my mortality when I began reporting on the death penalty. I was in my twenties, flush with life and baby children, measuring my days in month-by-month milestones and preschool birthday parties. Everything felt fresh and possible, and I had very little inkling that anything would ever feel any different. It seems that way when you and your children are young—that life is a long summer day never quite sloping into afternoon. I gave very little thought, and no serious contemplation, to the idea that any of it would ever come to an end.

In fact, part of what attracted me to the subject of capital punishment was that it intersected with my personal life and history not at all. In the early part of my career, writing as a young woman had required a degree of self-disclosure and personal engagement in both the content of my work and the promotion of it on social media that I had come over time to regret. Nevertheless I liked my work; I just came to a realization not too long ago that it ought not generally be about me. One of the great benefits of being a reporter is having free license to peer into other lives, after all, and I began to exercise that license with special verve.

But whose lives to present for national attention? I had always had a civic interest in capital punishment—in a democracy, state killing carries the imprimatur of the people, which implicates all of *us* whether we like it or not— but I also found (and continue to find) the problems of death row prisoners some of the most compelling in the country. Justified or not, these people are facing death; the fact that their killers are vested with legitimate power only adds to their difficulties. From the mere perspective of a reporter hoping to tell important, vital stories, no population had better cause to warrant attention than the men and women of death row.

So, I began the process of reaching out to prisoners with active cases through every available means: letters, telephone calls, contraband cellphone text exchanges, emails on prison-provided tablets, communications through lawyers. I was naive at the outset, though not in the traditional sense: I didn't believe, for instance, that everyone I encountered who purported to be innocent actually was (in fact, I have a preference for the confessed and admittedly guilty over the occasional innocence case, all else being equal, since we all already agree the innocent shouldn't be put to death); nor was I susceptible to the idea that everyone I met was merely wounded and in need of my nurturing. But I did labor under the impression

A

that these lives were so radically different from my own that I needn't take special care to maintain a professional detachment from them, and I was wrong.

I witnessed my first execution in 2020, then another in 2021, then attended the autopsy of a man executed under suspicious circumstances and served as an execution witness twice more in 2022. What began as a natural outgrowth of the beat—if you're going to cover capital punishment, you ought to become acquainted with exactly what it is—became, over time, something of a calling. On the first occasion, I had no prior knowledge of the prisoner nor any contact with him; on the second, I was in touch with prison staff who were speaking with the man as the day approached and even submitted a list of questions for him but never spoke directly with him. But then came the autopsy in Alabama: As I explain at greater length in these pages, that investigation revealed a pervasive corruption at the heart of the state's capital punishment regime and raised the stakes of the executions it planned to carry out next. By the time Alabama scheduled the execution of Alan Miller, it was in no mood to so much as answer my emails. I wouldn't be able to cover their next act as a media witness—I would have to contact Miller himself and serve as a personal witness.

This time, I came much closer to my subjects: As you will read, I was with Miller's family and his attorney the night the state tried and stunningly failed to kill him, a surreal and sadistic affair that began at a slot machine casino and ended in a hospital parking lot in the small hours of the morning, in a rendezvous with a prison warden and the local police. And, though the state had just botched one execution and completely failed another, Alabama scheduled another man, Kenneth "Kenny" Smith, to be executed following Miller. I met Smith just as he was given notice of his impending execution and communicated with him and his family over the weeks preceding his date. I wanted to understand the experience of a condemned person as their sentence went into effect— to document not just the culmination of capital punishment but its long and torturous buildup.

Kenny was remarkably frank about his condition, which was a brutal and equalizing one: No matter who you once were, a human sameness emerges in the shadow of death. He wasn't a monster, and he wasn't alone. He had a wife and children who were preparing to be bereaved, and they were guilty of nothing—to be punished for nothing. Kenny's date was close to the holidays, and I tried not to talk about the things he wouldn't be here for. I didn't think of them much myself, either.

It wasn't so much that I had become attached to him as I had become painfully empathetic with his situation— with the great brevity of all things and the ultimate reality of death, the blank gaping finality of it. The difference between Kenny and I—or Kenny and you, Kenny and anyone—was just that he *knew* his date. But we've all got one. And for the first time in my life, I saw with perfect clarity that day turns into night, and that death comes on a pale horse: All this is guaranteed, and I was no exception, and nor was anyone I loved. Everything suddenly felt incredibly dear—every evening when I kissed my children goodnight, couldn't it be the last, and oughtn't I bear that in mind?—but impossibly so.

Kenny, like Miller, survived his execution. But Alabama is not necessarily finished making attempts on his life, which has tempered my relief with a lingering concern. So it went with my recently acquired fear of death—which matured into a mellower, lower-intensity rumination over time. Friends of mine who had identified my late preoccupation with death—my early thirties "Memento Mori" moment—as a crisis of faith took heart in the fact that Miller and Kenny had lived, and I did too. In life, as in capital punishment, one has to learn to get by with strange victories.

Learning to pay adequate respect to death may be one of those. The stress suffered by a prisoner faced with imminent execution is, in my view, genuinely unsurpassed in terms of psychological torture. But the broader recognition of death—certain, imminent, and violent in the prisoner's case but distant, abstract, and natural in the free man's imagination—felt finally to me like the arrival of a certain season, the first sensible talk of autumn in the summertime of my life. I took the opportunity to get my affairs in order—just in case—and to plan seriously with my husband not just for an untimely loss in our household but for the aging of our parents. If I am not quite the same as I was before embarking on this reporting—a little more cautious, a little less frivolous—I owe it to death and consider it a favor.

I hope you will find something of value as well in these pages.

ELIZABETH BRUENIG

May 2023

A

A GOOD MAN, AT ONE TIME

———————

March 2022

BY THE TIME DAVID NEAL COX's life was put to an end last fall by the state of Mississippi, the man had become a rarity among death-row prisoners—a jailhouse advocate for his own execution. Some in that unusual tradition have had an agenda, such as Timothy McVeigh, who expected his 2001 death to become a symbol of federal brutality; others, including another Mississippian, Bobby Wilcher, who was killed in 2006, waived their appeals in a fit of pique or despair and then died trying to reinstate their pathways to survival. But not Cox. No ardent supporter of capital punishment could have found their passion for the practice better matched, or their reasoning for it better embodied, than in the 50-year-old man's rawboned frame.

The state of Mississippi wanted Cox dead, and Cox did too. In the days leading up to his death, the family of Cox's victims—people who were once related to Cox himself—told reporters that Cox was evil; that if he were ever free, he would kill again; and that his execution would bring closure to their beleaguered clan.

Cox had earned their hatred. Around dusk on a May 2010 evening in the northern Mississippi town of Sherman, Cox, armed with a .40-caliber handgun, shot his way inside a trailer in search of his estranged wife, Kim. Cox was apoplectic. He had spent nine months in the Pontotoc County Jail, after being arrested on charges of statutory rape, sexual battery, child abuse, and drug-possession offenses related to crystal meth. The victim of his alleged sexual predation was Lindsey Kirk, his 12-year-old stepdaughter, whom he had raised since she was 2. Cox blamed Kim for his incarceration because she told the police that her daughter had been abused. A few weeks out of jail on bond, Cox had come for revenge.

He had set out with enough ammunition to kill not only Kim but her father and stepmother, Benny and Melody Kirk, and her sister, Kristie Salmon, with whom she was staying. Benny and Melody were, mercifully, miles away at the time. Kristie managed to escape the hellish scene, along with Cox and Kim's 7-year-old son. Only Kim, Lindsey, and the couple's other son, who was 8, remained trapped inside.

First, Cox shot Kim twice, once in the arm and once through the abdomen—an injury that, a local surgeon told the jury at Cox's trial, likely generated agonizing pain as the contents of the intestines spilled into the abdominal cavity during the several hours it took Kim to bleed to death. The greater torture is harder to quantify: In a taped

A

interview reviewed by the jurors, Lindsey recounts that after Cox shot her mother, he forced the young girl to undress and then sexually assaulted her while Kim looked on, helpless. Lindsey struggled to tell the story through tears, indicating where on her body Cox had touched her as her mother lay dying.

Over the course of approximately eight hours, police gathered outside the trailer and attempted to negotiate with Cox. Occasionally, he would take to the telephone to spew poison at the police (if law enforcement tried to breach the premises, he warned, he would be "going for head shots") or at Benny, Kim's father, whom he seemed to delight in tormenting with details of his daughter's imminent death, at one point informing Benny that Kim was "bleeding like a stuck pig." On the phone, Cox told his sister Sharlott's husband that he had a bullet for Lindsey and another for himself, and yet that isn't how the assault came to an end: Eventually, around 3:30 in the morning, a SWAT team stormed the trailer. The officers rescued Lindsey and her half-brother and arrested Cox. Kim was already dead.

Cox pleaded guilty to charges of capital murder, sexual battery, burglary, kidnapping, and firing into a dwelling. If he meant to avoid the death penalty with a swift and complete admission of guilt, he failed. In September 2012, the jury returned a unanimous verdict sentencing Cox to death.

For a time, it seemed as though Cox would, like most prisoners condemned to die, fight his fate. In 2016, his attorneys began filing the sundry motions associated with post-conviction relief. But by the summer of 2018, Cox had begun communicating directly with the Mississippi Supreme Court, sending handwritten letters demanding that his lawyers be fired and all appeals be waived. Cox had come to a new faith, he said, and he wanted to die as soon as possible.

"I seek in earnest to wave all my appeals immediately, I seek to be executed as I do here this day stand on MS Death row a guilty man worthy of death," he wrote. Spiritual awakening notwithstanding, Cox was unrepentant. "If I had my perfect way & will about it," he wrote, "Id ever so gladly dig my dead sarkastic wife up of in whom I very happily & premeditatedly slaughtered on 5-14-2010 & with eager pleasure kill the fat heathern hore again." When overt hostility failed to elicit the instantaneous response Cox was looking for, he offered a constitutional plea. "I am Anabaptist," he wrote some weeks later, "namely, old order Amish, & it is in conflict with my religeon to have lawyers."

Five days later, Cox's lawyers filed a motion to retract all of Cox's efforts to waive his appeals. Cox had been extremely depressed when he sent the letters, they wrote, but he had since spoken with them and changed his mind about his situation.

This didn't last, however. In November 2018, Cox wrote again to the court, insisting anew on his desire to die. "I am worthy of death & I do not wish to challenge the State of Mississippi any further," he said. "I seek to bring clousure to my victims & family & all I hurt whether it be emotionally, phsyikally or both, by the speedy execution of my guilty body." A couple of days later, Cox explained in a handwritten affidavit that he had withdrawn his earlier pleas to live because he suffered a divided existence, torn between two parts of himself, which he described as "skin #1" and "skin #2." "Skin #1 seeks life & relief," Cox wrote, while "skin #2 seeks death & relief, still."

Cox's second skin won out. And despite the alarming impression that his declaration of a split psyche gave about his mental state, the Mississippi Supreme Court found him competent to waive his appeals. In October 2021, the court obliged Cox and set a date for his execution.

IN COURT OPINIONS PERTAINING TO COX, Mississippi's jurists appear largely incurious about what, precisely, had motivated the man to campaign for his own death. Maybe that sort of thing lay beyond their purview. The state had already condemned Cox to die, after all, so the termination of his appeals was, in all likelihood, just a matter of quibbling over time.

Still, I was intrigued by Cox's death-row volunteerism. There is an old adage, often attributed to Samuel Johnson, that the sight of the gallows clears the mind. With the total and irrevocable finality of death imminent, priorities fall into their proper place, pride and bluster wither away, and people begin to act rationally.

Yet Cox's proffered motives for seeking out his end didn't seem to me to reflect anything of the sort. In fact, they implied the opposite: that the possibility of hastening his own demise had motivated Cox to concoct lies and cruelties and misdirections, all with the goal of dying, which he felt was a better immediate prospect than the others available to him. His rationale was never coherent; his statements about his decision were contradictory. Yet he had a clear aim in mind. Why else would someone in one breath boast that they would "with eager pleasure" kill their victim again, and in the next express a desire to provide closure to that same victim's family in partial redress for emotional injury?

There was something else that could have—should have—been of interest to a Mississippi jurist with a real and heartfelt concern for justice. Cox had long been suspected of involvement in another disturbing incident, still unresolved. His brother's wife, Felecia Cox, had been missing since July 2007. According to Felecia's daughter, Amber Miskelly, Felecia disappeared while visiting Kim, a beloved friend, and it was Kim who filed the missing-person report. Miskelly told me she had suspected for years that Cox knew more about her mother's whereabouts than he let on, and had even written letters to him in prison begging him for information.

Miskelly told me that she was 18 years old and pregnant with her first child when her mother went missing. Her mom knew she had a grandchild on the way, Miskelly said, which is how "I knew she wouldn't just leave." So Miskelly searched for Felecia, whom she described as kind and loving—"my best friend"—for some 14 years. It was a painful, aching loss, kept fresh by uncertainty. But if Cox knew anything about Felecia's fate, he had never confessed.

Miskelly was distressed by the news that the court had agreed to execute Cox. "I thought I had more time to try to figure out—or at least contact David myself or something," she told a local news station.

If anyone was ever going to learn what had happened to Felecia or the location of her remains, Miskelly thought, it would come down to Cox himself, and the bloody war between his two skins.

AND SO I TURNED UP in Mississippi on November 17 to see David Cox die.

The execution arrived at a tense moment in the national debate over the death penalty. Roughly three weeks earlier, Oklahoma had executed a 60-year-old prisoner named John Marion Grant using a three-drug cocktail beginning with midazolam, a sedative. Grant's death did not go as planned. While media witnesses looked on, the man heaved, convulsed, and vomited before finally succumbing to the other drugs in the triad—vecuronium bromide, a paralytic, and potassium chloride, which stops the heart.

Grant's torturous death inflamed a years-long battle over whether lethal injection, in any of its many forms, is the humane and scientifically sound method of execution that its supporters claim it is. And while capital-defense attorneys across the country anxiously reviewed their clients' cases in light of Grant's misfortune, Mississippi openly planned to proceed with Cox's execution using the very same drug protocol.

Cox was to be killed at the Mississippi State Penitentiary, in Sunflower County, about a two-hour drive from Memphis. The prison, better known as Parchman Farm, sits near the center of the Mississippi Delta, some 7,000 square miles of broad, flat, rich-soiled floodplain.

Cox grew up in the northeastern corner of the state, the tail end of Appalachia. He was born to a 41-year-old mother of four; a sister, Sharlott, followed a year later. Before the girl was born, Cox's father left the family. From then on, Sharlott stated in a sworn affidavit, their mother worked multiple jobs, as a nursing-home cleaner, a school-cafeteria worker, and an aide to the elderly. Money was tight and occasionally absent altogether. Cox's mother

A

seems to have relied on the kindness of kin with mixed success. When the family's utilities were shut off, Sharlott recalled, their church raised money to cover the bill. When, one day, Cox and Sharlott arrived home on the school bus to find their mother standing newly evicted at the end of their driveway, the trio walked 15 miles to their aunt Myrtis's house, Cox told a social worker during a series of interviews in October 2018. They were permitted to sleep on a mattress in the chicken house adjacent to the hog and hen enclosures, where sun and rain fell intermittently through a hole in the roof. On starry nights, Cox recalled, his mother would drag the mattress underneath the hole and the three would gaze up together at the spangled Mississippi sky.

An itinerant and impoverished childhood gave way to an adolescence rife with substance abuse, neglect, and despair. Cox, who had been placed in special-education classes in elementary school, dropped out in seventh grade. By then, he had already been huffing gasoline on a daily basis for years, a habit that would persist into his adulthood. When he huffed, he told the social worker, he was "no longer a pissed off loner, I was no longer hungry, was no longer ugly," and he "loved the feeling of not being me." Cox and Sharlott sometimes stayed at their father's house, where Cox alleged that he witnessed his father sexually abusing his sister on at least one occasion. Their mother, Cox recounted, feared informing social services out of concern that the children might be put into foster care due to the family's abject poverty. Cox left home at 19 to work on a farm; by age 25, he had become a commercial truck driver.

I thought of Cox's life on the road during the drive south from Memphis. Maybe he once worked routes like these, where raw cotton fibers blow back from great heaping bales stacked on the beds of semitrucks crisscrossing the Delta. It would have been his last taste of real freedom, his closest brush with clean living. According to a sworn affidavit by Ricky McCain, Cox's first cousin, Cox was happy behind the wheel of his truck. "David loved being on the road," McCain said, "and would want to get back on the truck as soon as he could."

In 1995, while pulling a short-block engine from his pickup, Cox injured his back, which required surgery and, naturally, postoperative opioids. In 2003, a driver rear-ended Cox, further damaging his back. Another surgery, more pills, and disability benefits followed. By 2005, Cox was addicted to meth and cooking his own supply.

Cox had met Kim Kirk several years earlier. The two had married in 2000, and had two sons. Cox told the social worker who interviewed him in prison that he loved being a father, though he and Kim disagreed about how to raise the boys, leading to marital discord.

In April 2009, Kim and Lindsey left the home they shared with Cox and the boys to live for a time with Kim's cousin Brandy. Cox looked after the couple's sons, stewing in suspicion that Kim was cheating on him. In July of that year, Cox told the social worker, Kim called Cox in tears, asking to come home; Cox agreed that she and Lindsey could return. But before they did, Lindsey confided to Kim that Cox had raped her. Kim reported the allegation immediately, and Cox was arrested and incarcerated at the Pontotoc County Jail in August 2009, a turn of events that infuriated him. Cellmates of Cox's would later testify that he repeatedly vowed to kill Kim during his stint inside. In April 2010, Cox made bond. Weeks later, Kim was dead.

The night before Cox's execution, Melody Kirk, Kim's stepmother, told me that he had always been an "outdoor person," and that he likely hated being trapped inside. As the prison came into view, it occurred to me that the grand openness of the roads that once signaled freedom for him must now feel like a mockery of the same. The fields stretching for miles on either side of the highway had long been picked clean. A man would find it hard to escape from Parchman. The horizon would give him up.

INSIDE PARCHMAN FARM'S visitors' center—a white, windowless, barnlike building surrounded by a chain-link fence—I sat with a handful of local media personnel at two-seater tables facing a platform with a lectern, awaiting an address from Burl Cain, the commissioner of the Mississippi Department of Corrections.

Cain took to the podium at 4:47 p.m. to answer the press's questions. A former warden of the Louisiana State Penitentiary at Angola, infamously known as "The Farm," Cain is himself something of an institution. His tenure at Angola was long and exceptional, marked by the introduction of what Cain calls "moral rehabilitation"—the establishment of strong religious organizations to take the place of the unifying, anchoring, guiding presence otherwise supplied by gangs. Cain presided over occasional scandals and controversies at Angola too, including some of the sort one would associate with a large prison built on a former plantation, though he has denied any wrongdoing. According to Cain (but not his critics), his reign greatly diminished violence at the Farm. Now, at Parchman, he hopes to bring about a similar transformation.

He stood before us in a blue suit and blue-tinted aviators under a swoop of white hair. A local journalist asked Cain whether Cox had said anything about the possible location of Felecia Cox's body. Cain said he had confessed nothing, but noted that prison officials hadn't pressed him to. Another journalist asked who would claim Cox's body upon his death; Cain had no idea. Someone asked if Cox seemed remorseful.

"He is very, very remorseful," Cain said. Cain told us that he had shared Cox's last meal with him, a southern feast of fried catfish, french fries, coleslaw, and banana pudding. The man, Cain said, was "ready to go."

Later, sitting in the same small auditorium after Cox was dead, Cain would tell me that he had asked Cox about Felecia—at length, many times. And though Cox never said whether he had killed the woman, "he did tell us that he dug the grave . . . but he wouldn't tell us where." Cox seemed to have believed that if he explained the details of Felecia's death and burial, he'd have to live through another trial, delaying his death. With his execution in sight, he was unwilling to risk that.

I asked Cain why he thought Cox wanted so badly to die.

"He said to me the other day, 'I'm so tired of doing this. I need rest. I just need to rest,'" Cain said. He told me that Cox had become fervently religious in prison, a devout Anabaptist, as Cox had told the court, and that whatever hope he had for the future seemed to be invested in the next life. "David would say, 'I used to be a good man, but now I'm a real bad man' . . . He didn't like being a bad man. It was like—almost like he was demon-possessed."

Some evil is hard to explain in any other way. A few hours earlier, as we waited to be taken away to the execution chamber, I'd wondered whether Amber Miskelly would ever know what had happened to her mother. What reason would Cox have to tell anyone anything about a crime he had more or less gotten away with? Sometimes prisoners surrender bits of information about prior crimes during lengthy sentences in exchange for better conditions or other rewards; a canny convict might have gambled with the details of a past killing to delay his own death. But Cox showed no compunction about dying, rather the opposite. It was hard to stake much hope on the man's conscience.

AT 5:30 P.M., the media witnesses were led one by one into a staging area at the rear of the visitors' center, where we were parted from our phones, computers, and recorders, then given steno pads and pens. We waited on maroon vinyl-cushioned chairs in a tiled room like a church basement until a white prison van arrived to transport us to the execution chamber.

Night was falling. The van rolled along a few narrow back roads before arriving at Unit 17, where, under blazing-white floodlights, the death house is located. We were searched and patted down, then taken to the chamber itself.

We filed into a small, stuffy room fit with rows of folding chairs facing a window covered on the opposite side with a curtain. We were told not to speak. A row ahead, I saw two of Cox's long-suffering attorneys, Humphreys McGee and Treasure Tyson, both slump-shouldered and defeated. And then the curtain lifted away, revealing

A

David Neal Cox, already strapped to a gurney. A prison official asked an officer by the door of the witness room to hit the lights, and a murky dimness fell around us.

Cox looked peaceful, or resigned, or maybe just worn-out. As tall and lanky and awkwardly proportioned as ever, dressed in a red prison jumpsuit, a needle already in his arm. His hair was long, with a beard to match—maybe in accordance with his Old Order Amish inclinations—wiry and gray, speckled with white. The prison's superintendent lowered a microphone so Cox could deliver his last words.

"I want my children to know that I love them very much," he said, "and that I was a good man, at one time. And don't ever read anything but the King James Bible. And I wanna thank the commissioner for being so kind to me. And that's all I got to say."

Later, press reports would note that Cox's final words contained not a hint of remorse. But perhaps he had already expressed it. Cain told me that Cox's 18-year-old son, whom he had last seen fleeing from the trailer as a boy, had come to see him that day, something Cox had been anxiously hoping for. Cain told me that Cox had said to his son, "I wish I hadn't done what I did. I wish I hadn't done it. I wish I hadn't taken your mama away from you."

Not that what he had to say mattered; it wasn't as though any expression of regret could have redeemed him, not then. Nor had Cox ever been good at finding the right words. Humphreys McGee told me that Cox had hated himself, that he had insulted his own intelligence frequently, his inability to express himself, to say what he meant to.

They don't tell you when they start the poison drip; it just begins. You can see the changes, though, in the person. Sometime after six, Cox took a few labored breaths, and his lips worked fruitlessly for a moment or two. His skin began to appear livid to me then, shades of violet settling near his ears. And then a long stillness. A woman with a stethoscope stepped forward and declared Cox's time of death to be 6:12 p.m. The curtain dropped, the lights came on, and they herded us back to the van.

I READ THE STATEMENT Cox's attorneys issued after his death the next day, as I traveled home. Cox had asked his lawyers to say that the "inhumane prison conditions at Parchman" had factored into his decision to give up his appeals. Vermin ran rampant inside the prison walls, Cox told McGee: rats, mice, spiders, cockroaches, snakes, opossums. There was no air-conditioning during the long southern summers. The humidity control was so poor, Cox said, that when it rained outside, "it rained inside," with water falling from the ceiling. (Cain says that most buildings in the prison are now air-conditioned and have undergone cleaning and repairs.)

I thought of Cox peering up at the stars through the hole in that chicken coop he'd lived in with his mother and sister, with the fowl and pigs squawking and shuffling nearby. Everything had ended more or less the way it had begun for him: misery to misery, isolation to isolation, dust to dust.

I went home. The holidays arrived. Cox haunted my thoughts. McGee had told me that Cox had said he wanted to die so he could experience something in the next life that he couldn't in this one. He recalled how Cox had reminded him to treasure his family and friends, because he himself had lost all of those relationships—or destroyed them. "And I didn't contradict him," McGee said. "I wanted to tell him, 'You do have friends.' But I just let him talk."

In the end, the monster of North Mississippi was a wizened, miserable old man, alone in the world and hounded by guilt and shame and ceaseless pain. Cox had never wanted to be himself—hardly anyone had ever seemed to want him for any reason at all—and the American criminal-justice system had only confirmed what he had perhaps always known: that he was worthless, his life was worthless, there was nothing in him of any value to anyone, and the only good he could do, even for his own children, was to die. Much of his personal hell was of his own making, and he had no fixed presumption as to whether the next life would hold more or less of the same.

Still, Cox's better skin spared time for one last act. On October 26, after the court had set a date for his execution, he drew a map of the area near his mobile home where he had buried the body of Felecia Cox. He attached a waiver permitting his attorneys to share the information after his death, and mailed the documents to their office, trusting that they would disclose what he had asked. And then, a day before his execution, he dictated a letter for his attorneys to transcribe and deliver to Amber Miskelly. He apologized "for taking your mom away." Roughly a month after Cox was killed, on December 12, Felecia's remains were recovered from the site Cox had indicated.

Felecia hadn't done anything wrong, Cox said in his final dictation. He said that her death was senseless. He said that he shouldn't have harmed her. He said that he prayed for forgiveness.

A

CAN AMERICA KILL ITS
PRISONERS KINDLY?

March 2022

WHETHER KILLING A PERSON VIA intravenous poisoning qualifies as cruel and unusual remains, for the moment, an open question. Beginning in late February, the United States District Court for the Western District of Oklahoma heard testimony at the trial of *Glossip v. Chandler,* an eight-year-old lawsuit filed on behalf of a group of death-row inmates that seeks to prove that Oklahoma's current lethal-injection recipe—500 milligrams of midazolam, followed by 100 milligrams of vecuronium bromide, followed by 240 mEq potassium chloride—violates the Constitution's Eighth Amendment ban on cruel and unusual punishment. The case focuses on the constitutionality of midazolam, a sedative with limited anesthetic and no analgesic properties that critics argue results in slow and painful deaths for those poisoned with it.

Recent events have lent the case a special urgency. Last year, John Marion Grant was discovered to have inhaled his own vomit before dying once Oklahoma authorities had injected him with the midazolam-led cocktail, a death that witnesses described as particularly gruesome. Nevertheless, another three executions deploying the same method have gone forward since Grant's.

The suit will be the latest and most noteworthy in a lengthy lineage of so-called method-of-execution litigation, or legal challenges to capital sentences under the Eighth Amendment. In some states, evidence that lethal injection is inhumane has already led to de facto shutdowns of execution chambers—California, for instance, hasn't attempted an execution since a sprawling 2006 method-of-execution lawsuit unearthed disturbing facts about the state's protocol. *Glossip* probably can't bank on similar results in Oklahoma, a deep-red state. But that doesn't mean the lawsuit has no chance of making a difference for Americans on death row.

Success for a suit like *Glossip*—only the latest development in a body of litigation that has changed capital punishment in America by demanding justice in how the state kills—is a funny thing. Method-of-execution challenges serve an obvious and necessary constitutional function, forcing states to (at least attempt to) keep pace with the "evolving standards of decency" test that the Supreme Court has built into the meaning of the Eighth Amendment. Yet the result of so many decades of method challenges is the lethal-injection regime of the modern era—which, per *Glossip*, has hardly resolved the inhumane nature of American executions. Therein lies a surreal backwardness: A win for the prisoners in *Glossip* wouldn't mean an end to Oklahoman executions, just a ban on midazolam; killings might become marginally more humane, but they also might not—in fact, matters in the future may well be *worse*. As cases like *Glossip* multiply and lethal injection becomes a more difficult proposition for states across the board, the legal push for executions that comport with the Eighth Amendment may well result in the resurrection of bygone methods of last resort—the firing squad, electric chair, or gas chamber, with the perverse result that prisoners' battle for their constitutional rights will, in the hands of the state, become an assault on the very same.

The professor and legal scholar John Bessler writes in his careful history of the Eighth Amendment that America's ban on cruel and unusual punishment began in part with the case of Titus Oates, an English clergyman who received an excessive (and elaborate) punishment for perjury, making him a cause célèbre among 17th-century British elites and igniting outrage toward King James II. Oates's aristocratic defenders, inspired by the foment, threw their support behind the English Bill of Rights' proscription of cruel and unusual punishments, including brutal forms of physical torture as well as exorbitant fines.

Roughly a century later, Bessler told me, the Framers of the American Constitution ratified the ideals set forth in the English Bill of Rights in our own founding documents, in the form of the Eighth Amendment. By the following century, Deborah Denno, a professor at Fordham University School of Law, told me, method-of-execution challenges were already being brought under the amendment's auspices.

"They started right away with electrocution in the late 1800s," Denno said. She pointed to the case of William Kemmler, a murderer in New York State condemned to be the first American to be executed by electrocution, in 1890, as the beginning of method challenges in the United States. Kemmler lost his challenge—but, Denno said, his death still marked a turning point in the history of capital punishment. His horrific execution (one witness commented on the "terrible stench" of burning hair and flesh that flooded the chamber as the current coursed through Kemmler) proved the electric chair effective, and attorneys around the country had what they needed to challenge the method in court.

"Those challenges are what start leading us to other methods of execution," Denno said. The electric chair, a technological marvel, had been introduced to replace the grisly spectacle of hanging—yet it, too, resulted in more than its fair share of needless agony and stomach-churning gore. Tied up in court battles about the legality of their methods, states continued to search for newer, more modern forms of killing—the sort that worked quickly and came with minimal body fluids that might give onlookers

A

the impression that putting a person to death is a somewhat cruel affair.

Lethal injection, legalized in 1977 and first used by the state of Texas to execute a man in 1982, initially seemed to have solved the death penalty's public relations problem by introducing a way of killing people with nary a drop of blood nor a wisp of smoke. But, as the Berkeley Law School criminologist Franklin E. Zimring noted in his 1986 book, *Capital Punishment and the American Agenda*, within nine years of its development, lethal injection had already collapsed the "fantasy that the intentional taking of human life could be made acceptable to modern standards of decency by changing the means of execution." In other words, poisoning people to death turned out to be neither as simple nor as painless as its proponents had perhaps imagined.

But even so, the needle gained widespread acceptance, Denno told me, and prosecutors soon found themselves in a bind. "By 2008, just about all the states now had lethal injection," she told me. "So the rub is, when lethal injection is challenged, [prosecutors] don't have another method of execution to go to . . . And by that time, you had a bunch of very sophisticated attorneys who were on to these execution-method arguments." Denno said that as a result, by the late aughts, "it looked like all these challenges were shutting down states' abilities to execute anybody."

While litigation challenging lethal injection's constitutionality percolated through the courts, those facing execution and their attorneys could indulge in a little uneasy relief: If the method were legally unsettled, then prison authorities were unlikely to move forward, or so it seemed. One method-of-execution challenge, initially filed in 2005 as *Roane v. Gonzales,* halted federal executions for 15 years as attorneys produced expert testimony and evidence and Department of Justice officials struggled to obtain certain lethal chemicals. One could be forgiven for having believed, just for a little, that the American death penalty was simply dying the way it mandated killing: quietly, privately, paralyzed in the hands of professionals.

The reality is that lethal injection falls short of the replicable accuracy we might expect of medical procedures, and the courts are aware of that. To give one example of a factor that limits the predictability of the method, in a 2019 memorandum, Steven Engel, an assistant attorney general in the Trump administration, concluded that the Food and Drug Administration lacks the authority to regulate chemicals to be used for lethal injections, because the *intent* is to use them to kill, meaning there's no way to find them "safe and effective" in the traditional sense. Further, each state sets its own standards for carrying out executions—and fails to meet them in their own ways. A

A

2006 investigation into California's death chambers found, for instance, that the lights were kept so dim to protect the identity of prison staff involved with executions that it was unlikely that employees could reliably see what they were doing; that same year, a doctor who supervised lethal injections testified that he was dyslexic and admitted that he sometimes confused the names of medications or the numbers involved in properly dosing them. And accidents do happen: As recently as 2015, an Oklahoma prisoner was killed with the wrong chemical.

Even if there were some way to guarantee that lethal-injection drugs were well regulated and staff were expertly trained in administering them, it would still remain the case that pharmaceutical companies are hesitant to manufacture and sell said chemicals to states for use in executions, thanks to their own ethical concerns and the protests of anti-death-penalty activists. Thus states must still cast about for whatever deadly chemicals they can scrounge up—which leaves the tax-paying public entirely in the dark as to where its money is being spent. In 2017, running short on midazolam, the director of the Arkansas Department of Corrections purchased 40 vials of the chemical for $250 in cash from an unnamed source. In Idaho, correctional officials were accused *once again* this year of hauling a suitcase full of money to a parking lot for a similar handoff. And in Arizona, authorities spent roughly a million during a budget squeeze on pentobarbital in unmarked jars to be delivered to an undisclosed location by an unnamed supplier.

Naturally, these irregularities have drawn the attention of journalists, to the profound displeasure of capital-punishment states nationwide. "Since January 2011," a 2018 report from the Death Penalty Information Center noted, "legislatures in thirteen states have enacted new secrecy statutes that conceal vital information about the execution process. Of the seventeen states that have carried out 246 lethal-injection executions between January 1, 2011, and August 31, 2018 . . . fourteen states prevented witnesses from seeing at least some part of the execution. Fifteen prevented witnesses from hearing what was happening inside the execution chamber. None of the seventeen allowed witnesses to know when each of the drugs was administered."

These are all troublesome obstacles to grapple with if one is permitted to serve as a media witness at all. In Oklahoma, only journalists representing local, Oklahoma-based media outlets are permitted to witness executions; only locals are allowed, too, in Texas—where a plurality of U.S. executions occur—save for one slot reserved for the Associated Press. In Alabama, because of the coronavirus pandemic, only a single media witness has been permitted to watch as prison officials administer lethal injections. This means that large, national media outlets

A

have little opportunity to send their own journalists to observe state killings and report on what they see. When I began calling and writing to the Alabama Department of Corrections several weeks in advance of the scheduled execution of Matthew Reeves, who was killed in January, I hoped I might apply to fill the one spot. I never heard back at all.

What don't these states want you to see? Presumably what I witnessed during the federal execution of 56-year-old Alfred Bourgeois in 2020. Bourgeois's execution was occasioned by the Trump administration's secretive procurement of a stockpile of pentobarbital, which Attorney General William Barr directed the Bureau of Prisons to use to execute 13 people in the final months of Donald Trump's tenure. Several months later, after President Joe Biden had taken office and Attorney General Merrick Garland had issued a moratorium on federal executions, the U.S. District Court for the District of Columbia decided to proceed with discovery in *Roane v. Garland,* the current iteration of the very same method-of-execution lawsuit filed under *Roane v. Gonzales* back in 2005. Now the court is considering (among other deaths) whether Bourgeois suffered beyond what this country has chosen to countenance as he was put to death by lethal injection on December 11, 2020, in Indiana.

I was there that evening, only a few yards from Bourgeois. In the chamber with him was a handful of other people, including Jonathan Hemingway, a Federal Bureau of Prisons official who has already submitted his testimony in *Roane,* on behalf of the government. According to Hemingway's sworn testimony, Bourgeois never gave any indication of being in any pain or discomfort; he just drifted off into deep breaths and snores before peacefully passing away. Hemingway did briefly see Bourgeois's "stomach area moving up and down," though he emphasized a second time that the episode hadn't made him suspect distress.

I confess that I saw things differently. Like the rest of the media witnesses present, I was stationed in a room separated from the execution chamber by a concrete wall furnished with a one-way window. On the other side of the window was Bourgeois, strapped to a gurney; we witnesses gazed up at his face from below. The angle permitted an excellent view of Bourgeois's midsection. I watched as he took those effortful breaths with his mouth gaping wide. Then his gut began to churn.

Nobody who witnessed Bourgeois's death overlooked this sequence of convulsions, though some, as in Hemingway's case, characterized them as little more than slight changes in posture. In the throes of death, Bourgeois's midsection undulated with such an eerie, forceful pulse that it put me in mind of looking down at my belly nine months pregnant, when my children were as good as born but not quite and made uneasy peace with

A

captivity by rolling and stretching. But Bourgeois's spasms looked, even in the moment, like what I suspect they were: his musculature's effort to draw air into his lungs as he drowned in his own secretions. It was not a quick death.

That should matter. That John Marion Grant vomited repeatedly as he died should matter. In *Glossip,* it still might: If the suit is successful, midazolam may be found unconstitutional for use in lethal injections and purged from death chambers nationwide. The trial wrapped up earlier this month; a decision is expected as soon as mid-May, and the defense attorneys are hopeful. In such small increments is progress made.

Or, elsewhere, reversed: This year, prison officials in South Carolina announced the completion of a $53,600 overhaul of the state's execution facilities in preparation for potential killings by firing squad. Like many states, South Carolina has struggled for years to access the scarce lethal-injection drugs available for use. But the state also passed a law last year forcing condemned prisoners to choose an available execution method—either firing squad or the electric chair—should correctional officials prove unable to obtain the chemicals necessary for lethal injection. As of now, South Carolina hasn't scheduled any executions, by firing squad or another method. But the state is positioning itself to proceed with killings eventually.

Among all the amendments in the Bill of Rights, the Eighth may be the noblest, because it ensures the protection of condemned criminals, the most friendless and vulnerable people. And it should be vindicated, not only for their sake—though mainly so—but also for our own.

A

TWO EXECUTIONS ON A THURSDAY IN AMERICA

May 2022

ON A RECENT THURSDAY NIGHT in America, April 21, two different states planned to preside over the execution of two different men—Oscar Franklin Smith, 72, in Tennessee; and Carl Wayne Buntion, 78, in Texas—and yet, for similar reasons, neither plan went off precisely as expected.

Smith, who was sentenced to death in 1990 for the brutal slaying of his estranged wife and her two teenage sons, was meant to represent a return to lethal injection for the state of Tennessee, which executed its previous three death-row prisoners via electrocution. In fact, Tennessee has executed five people in its electric chair since 2018, mainly thanks to lethal injection's emergent reputation as a painful, lingering way to die. Prison officials had last carried out a lethal injection in 2019, on Donnie Edward Johnson—with disturbing results. In life, Johnson had been party to a legal challenge to the state's method of executing its wards, and in death, he appeared to vindicate those concerns. Johnson's attorney, who was present at the time of his killing, reported that "gurgling" and "coughing" noises issued from the man's throat as he died, potentially indicating pain as he struggled to breathe.

Nevertheless, Smith had elected to take his chances with the method. He had chosen the allotted $20 worth of food—a double bacon cheeseburger, deep-dish apple pie, and vanilla-bean ice cream—that would see him to his death. He had endured the fruitless pleas for mercy on his behalf that temporarily raise one's spirits and the repeated demands for blood that quiet all hope. And then, while receiving what he believed to be his final Holy Communion, Smith heard the shocking news that Governor Bill Lee had issued him a temporary reprieve, citing an unspecified "oversight in preparation for lethal injection."

While Smith reportedly slumped in relief in Tennessee, prison officials in Texas went busily ahead with their own work. Carl Wayne Buntion was sentenced to death in 1991 for the murder of a motorcycle-mounted police officer who had pulled over a car Buntion was riding in for a routine traffic violation. At 78, he was the oldest prisoner on Texas's death row, and was poised to become the oldest person executed by the state since the mid-1970s. Indeed, some combination of Buntion's lengthy imprisonment of more than 30 years, including 20 spent in solitary confinement, and his failing health (he used a wheelchair and

A

took several prescription heart medications) was evidently what Justice Stephen Breyer had in mind when he wrote that Buntion's case "calls into question the constitutionality of the death penalty" on Eighth Amendment grounds, "and reinforces the need for this Court, or other courts, to consider that question in an appropriate case."

With all of that in mind, one might assume that Texas authorities would have taken special care in their handling of Buntion's execution via lethal injection—and perhaps they did. But the state has also taken special care to hide much of its lethal-injection procurement procedures from the public, making ascertaining what the state's standards even are all but impossible, let alone determining whether they're generally followed. In 2015 the state passed a law shielding the identity of anyone who participates in or supplies materials for use in an execution, citing safety concerns. Since then, it has been enormously difficult for capital defense attorneys, advocates, or the press to keep tabs on precisely how Texas has been killing its citizens.

Nevertheless, largely thanks to lawsuits and Freedom of Information Act requests filed by activists, attorneys, and journalists over the years, we do have some insights into the particulars of Texas's executions. Specifically, we can assemble a decent picture of what Texas's supply of the lethal chemical pentobarbital looks like—or *looked* like, until the execution of Carl Buntion.

Prior to a scheduled lethal injection in Texas, an employee of the Texas Department of Criminal Justice typically communicates to the attorneys of the condemned prisoner some details about the chemicals selected for use in the person's execution, including the sizes and beyond-use dates of the vials (a date past which compounded pharmaceuticals ought not be used). Specifically, Texas stocks vials of its single lethal drug, pentobarbital, in two sizes: larger 5-gram vials containing 100 milliliters of the sedative, and smaller 2.5-gram vials containing 50 milliliters. Each execution requires 5 grams of pentobarbital to be injected, and 5 grams on hand as backup. This means that each execution expends either one larger vial or two smaller vials.

Over time, Texas's supply of pentobarbital has dwindled, leaving the state with enough of the chemical to kill 13 of its 197 death-row prisoners, three of whom already have upcoming execution dates. Why not refresh its stores with a trip to the pharmacy? Largely because most major pharmaceutical companies aren't interested in selling their products for use in executions. When the drug giant Pfizer banned the sale of its pharmaceuticals for lethal injections in 2016, it became the latest in a roster of more than 20 transatlantic firms to take the same course. Now, with more than 50 health-care companies worldwide having taken similar stances, lethal-injection drugs produced by

A

reliable, well-regulated drug makers have become something of an extinct commodity.

To preserve the remainder of its stock, Texas must carefully monitor the vials' expiration dates. Records show that to ensure that its drugs are still potent enough to be effective, Texas periodically sends sample vials from its stockpile for laboratory testing, and then returns them to storage. And while it's possible that Texas has found some way to secretly and swiftly source new pentobarbital, emails and storage logs I reviewed strongly suggest that the state has instead maintained some of its same small and diminishing stock of poison for nearly three years, extending beyond-use dates when possible via the retesting routine, in some cases up to five times. (A spokesperson for the Texas Department of Criminal Justice declined to answer questions about its pentobarbital inventory, citing state confidentiality law.) Attorneys for prisoners on death row have argued that using drugs so old could subject their clients to torturous pain due to the unpredictable effects that pharmaceuticals may have when used past their prime.

Evidently displeased with the scrutiny to which the state of their drug supply has been subjected recently, Texas made an unusual call in Buntion's case. Buntion's attorneys wrote in an emergency-reprieve request sent to Governor Greg Abbott that when they'd inquired about which vials of pentobarbital were being set aside to kill Buntion, an employee of the criminal-justice department replied, "The specifics regarding the pentobarbital intended to be administered to your client have not yet been determined." A week later, Buntion's lawyers told me, Texas still had not explained to them which vials were used to kill him, or why they'd declined to specify. (A spokesperson said the department has not released information about which vials were used to execute Buntion because it hasn't received an official request to do so.)

Tennessee, too, has refused to inform even Oscar Smith's counsel as to what "oversight" caused his execution to be disrupted by a last-minute (and temporary) reprieve. Kelley Henry, one of Smith's lawyers, told me that she had heard only rumors about why the state pulled back so suddenly, and that all of the rumors had to do with the condition of Tennessee's lethal-injection drugs. While Henry hopes to eventually learn more about what took place behind prison walls that Thursday evening, she told me she wasn't convinced anyone would ever know.

Secrecy, evasion, and the agnostic muteness of a redactor's black box—if you're looking for open, responsive, democratic governance, capital punishment is the wrong domain. What is known inspires misgivings about what isn't. With old drugs dripping through their fingers and older prisoners shuffling uneasily between their cells and the death chamber, capital states are in a strange position.

To some, these breakdowns in process and near-panicked reticence about what ought to be freely available information may suggest that we are living through the last gasps of lethal injection. But I worry that all of the carelessness, hastily imposed secrecy measures, and casual indifference to justice and suffering represent a darker reality: We are in fact living through lethal injection's heyday, witnessing it the way capital states would always like to carry it out— no oversight, no accountability, no survivors.

SHOULD THE PARKLAND
SHOOTER DIE?

August 2022

NIKOLAS CRUZ, 23, IS GUILTY OF murdering 17 people and injuring more with an AR-15 rifle at his former high school in Parkland, Florida, in February 2018. No one—not Florida prosecutors, not Cruz's defense team, not Cruz himself, who pleaded guilty to all charges levied against him—disputes those facts. On the contrary, Cruz recapitulated his guilt in each count of murder and attempted murder in court last October before issuing an apology for his crimes. "I am very sorry for what I did, and I have to live with it every day," he said, "and if I were to get a second chance, I would do everything in my power to try to help others."

Cruz's regrets, issued before the families of victims gathered in the courtroom, did little to ease survivors' grief and rage. The father of a 14-year-old girl murdered by Cruz dismissed the prisoner's repentance as "ridiculous" during an interview with NPR. Listening to prosecutors describe in detail how his child had been murdered was wrenching. "There is no way to hear about how many times your daughter was shot by a cold and calculating killer that is easy to take," he said. "It's . . . it was a very disturbing day."

It could've been among the last public recapitulations of the Valentine's Day murders at Marjory Stoneman Douglas High School. Cruz had pleaded guilty; his defense team had agreed to accept life without the possibility of parole. There was no need for a trial whatsoever. But prosecutors and some (though by no means all) survivors and survivors' families felt that leaving Cruz to die the slow and lonely deaths that men die in prison, amid rampant disease and sexual violence, would come up short of justice and that he had to be executed instead. And so Cruz's death-penalty sentencing trial began on July 18.

No penalty levied on Earth can answer the suffering of a parent wailing for her lost young. No punishment can fill the aching silence where the daily clamor of children used to be, or stir the brutal stillness they leave behind. Even if we were to set the price of one human life at another, capital punishment can't deliver justice for multiple murder victims—nor for the wounded survivors. If a man can kill a single person and receive the exact same punishment as a murderer who massacred more than a dozen, in what sense does execution represent a proportional sentence? This is to say: When, as I expect, the jury in Florida decides to put Cruz to death, it will not be justice even by the logic inherent to the death penalty itself. Nevertheless, the question of whether the state may kill Cruz is the only one that the trial in Florida seeks to resolve.

To kill Cruz, prosecutors will have to convince the jury that the aggravating factors in his case (the number of casualties, the atrocious cruelty of the killings, and the "cold, calculated, and premeditated manner" of the attack) outweigh any mitigating factors (the possibility of developmental problems related to drug and alcohol exposure in utero, a troubled upbringing, his history of self-harm and violence against others, and diagnoses of depression and autism). But winning death sentences is less about meeting any specific legal criteria than it is about getting the jury to hate the defendant. As with any persuasion campaign, graphic material is key.

Since Cruz's sentencing trial began, prosecutors have played cellphone videos shot by students during the massacre; shown security-camera footage of the murders; asked survivors to undress and display their scars, like holy martyrs, in open court; and taken testimony from witnesses and victims that has left survivors and their families distraught. During the screening of one cellphone clip, a relative of a murdered girl shouted for someone to stop the video; bailiffs hushed her.

Every jury trial is a show trial, and prosecutors are writers or directors, not performers. They draw memories and emotions from their witnesses to illustrate the scale of the killer's evil, but the brute strokes must still be sketched out by the grieving survivors themselves.

The trial of a school shooter is also a *production,* in that the process generates new material to build out the killer's legend. School shooters are so notoriously interested in memorializing their murders and the events leading up to them that public-safety campaigns and criminology researchers now widely recommend that journalists not name them in coverage at all. And yet, Cruz's trial is effectively packaging and advertising his very own basement tapes—the cellphone videos and social media posts that presaged his transformation into a murderer. They were public already, but are now even more deeply engraved in the hideous canon of infamous shooters. The prosecution's decision to illustrate Cruz's slaughter moment by moment, using all available footage, will supply plenty more chum for the internet's darkest waters. This phenomenon—the mass shooting as bildungsroman, the preservation and celebration of the killer's memoirs in his niche, memetic subculture—is both the chief goal of school shootings and the inspiration for copycat attacks. This isn't a possible interpretation of events, but a matter of fact.

That Cruz pleaded guilty and attempted to forgo the public spectacle of a trial, but was denied the attempt for the sake of capital punishment, is thus especially troubling. Obscurity would be a kind of surrender, in the context of his particular crime.

Cruz's defense team did not argue that he was not guilty by reason of insanity (though, to my mind, the young man's history very bluntly demonstrates that he's never sustained a significant period of rational behavior). That nuance will now be lost to many during his sentencing trial, when his defense team must elucidate after all his psychological and emotional difficulties.

The prosecutors, for their part, will have to do something philosophically interesting: prove that Cruz is—himself, in his own person, unmoved by madness and uncoerced by external forces—*entirely* culpable for his crimes. It cannot be that he is only, say, *somewhat* evil; it cannot be that he was largely warped by his moment in history and weakened by experiences or conditions that cannibalized what little fortitude he may have had. If that were the case, the jury would have to entertain the possibility that Cruz isn't *remarkably* evil, but is rather one in an ever-lengthening lineage of dangerously troubled young men with plenty of bad role models and easy access to high-capacity rifles and ammunition. What the relationship between those two realities is—whether Cruz deserves to live or die—is something I can scarcely comprehend and suspect only heaven knows. And yet, a jury of everyday Floridians is going to have to figure it out.

The rest of us—an American public regularly exposed to incomprehensibly horrific news—will be left by this prolonged, dramatically staged trial with a still-greater

A

catalog of the dying cries of gunned-down children. One mass shooting bleeds into another. Standing in the heat of a neighbor's garden the other evening, I mentioned that I was writing something—something about killing, someone who was killed or killed someone or is about to be killed—and my addled interlocutor begged pardon: *Is this Buffalo, or Uvalde, or the Fourth of July?* This is Parkland, I clarified—the Florida shooting from a while back. It's in the news again because they want to execute him.

She looked at me, bewildered, and I was suddenly struck by how heavy the news felt to bear, amid the welter of sweet honeysuckle and florid summer hydrangeas. I let the subject sink, sorry to have said anything. Still, for the shortest of seconds, I wondered if I should volunteer that I certainly wasn't defending him. And yet I do believe he ought to have a defense. And not just that: His defense ought to succeed—not because what he did is defensible, but because the state set out to destroy the only thing about the man worth defending at all.

DEAD TO RIGHTS

August 2022

THIS MUCH IS UNDISPUTED: In 1994, Joe Nathan James Jr. murdered Faith Hall, a mother of two he had formerly dated; in 1999, he was sentenced to death in Jefferson County, Alabama; and he was executed on July 28, 2022. Whether James ought to have been killed was and is, by contrast, deeply disputed—Hall's family pleaded that their mercy should spare him, and the state government acted against their wishes. Also disputed is the matter of how, exactly, the Alabama Department of Corrections took James's life. Or it was in my mind, at least, until I saw what they had done to him, engraved in his skin.

A little over a week ago, James's body lay on a bloody shroud draped over an exam table in an Alabama morgue scarcely large enough to accommodate the three men studying the corpse. He had been dead for several days, but there was still time to discover what exactly had happened to him during the roughly three-hour period it took to—in the Department of Corrections' telling—establish access to a vein so an execution team could deliver the lethal injection of drugs that would kill him.

Despite the long delay and an unnaturally short execution, the Department of Corrections had assured media witnesses gathered to observe James's death that "nothing out of the ordinary" had happened in the course of killing the 50-year-old. It was suspicion of that claim that led to this private autopsy.

By the time I arrived at the morgue where Joel Zivot, an associate professor of anesthesiology and surgery at Emory University and a lethal-injection opponent, had agreed to join a local independent pathologist named Boris Datnow and his assistant, Jay Glass, James's body had undergone days of postmortem swelling in cool storage. Datnow would later caution me about the difficulty of our inquiry—the edema had diminished our chances of locating punctures left by needles during the execution—though my initial impression of James was of someone whose hands and wrists had been burst by needles, in every place one can bend or flex. That and the carnage farther up one arm told a radically different tale than the narrative offered by the Alabama Department of Corrections, even to the naked eye. Something terrible had been done to James while he was strapped to a gurney behind closed doors without so much as a lawyer present to protest his treatment or an advocate to observe it, yet the state had insisted that nothing unusual had taken place. Approached for comment about the allegations contained in this article, Department of Corrections officials declined to speak with me.

Obdurate disregard for genuine inquiries seems to be the state's disposition where capital punishment is concerned. In the months prior to James's execution, Faith Hall's brother Helvetius and her two daughters, Terrlyn and Toni, lobbied Governor Kay Ivey to spare the man's life, repeatedly stating that they had forgiven James and had no desire to see him killed. (The Halls, like James, are Black.) Nevertheless, the execution, scheduled for 6 p.m., went ahead unhindered, with Ivey explaining her office's disregard for the victim's family's wishes as a matter of principle.

When members of the media who had been selected to witness James's execution arrived for their transport to William C. Holman Correctional Facility's death chamber, two female journalists, the Associated Press's Kim Chandler and AL.com's Ivana Hrynkiw, were subjected to dress-code checks by prison staff, who demanded that Hrynkiw change from a skirt into a borrowed pair of men's fishing waders and sneakers before allowing her to proceed as a witness. By the time everyone was shod and appareled to the DOC's specifications and loaded onto prison transport vans, it was 6:33 p.m. (I had contacted the agency about applying to witness James's execution, but had been ignored.)

And then, media witnesses reported, they waited—for hours. Prisoners on Holman's death row held up signs—a captive message from a captive audience—stating that the victim's family didn't want James dead, that this was a murder. Time passed, then more: Finally, around 9:00, roughly three hours after the scheduled time of execution, media witnesses were led into the execution chamber.

I have witnessed two executions, and in both cases the men were alert and responsive to corrections staff in the moments prior to lethal injection. After all, multidrug cocktails including paralytics and sedatives only begin to affect a person's consciousness *after* administration. Before the injections begin, the men I've seen die have spoken at least briefly of love and regret. But James neither responded to his death warrant nor gave any last words—not even a refusal to offer a final statement, per Kim Chandler. In fact, witnesses, including Chandler and Hrynkiw, reported that James's eyes stayed closed during the entire procedure, flickering only in his death throes, and that he remained unresponsive from beginning to end. His death warrant was read at 9:03 p.m., the lethal drugs began to flow at 9:04, and he was declared dead, finally, at 9:27.

What happened to James during the three-hour interval between his scheduled execution and his time of death, and why was he apparently unconscious in the execution chamber? The Alabama DOC gave the gathered reporters no explanation for the long delay, or for his strange demeanor in the chamber. Pressed for an explanation by journalists on the scene that night, John Hamm, the corrections department commissioner, said, in somewhat scattered fashion, that he couldn't "overemphasize this process. We're carrying out the ultimate punishment, the execution of an inmate. And we have protocols and we're very deliberate in our process, and making sure everything goes according to plan. So if that takes a few minutes or a few hours, that's what we do."

Subsequent official statements only confused matters further. For instance, DOC spokesperson Kelly Betts wrote in an email to members of the media that "ADOC's execution team strictly followed the established protocol. The protocol states that if the veins are such that intravenous access cannot be provided, the team will perform a central line procedure. Fortunately, this was not necessary and with adequate time, intravenous access was established." Eventually, the DOC conceded that it could not confirm whether James had been "fully conscious" during the lethal-injection procedure, though it assured journalists that he had not been sedated.

Aside from the DOC, nobody seemed especially satisfied with that account of events. Jim Ransom, the last of many defense attorneys to represent James, was especially disturbed when he heard that his client hadn't responded to the warden's prompt to offer his last words. "That sent up red flags. It didn't ring true," Ransom told me the night of the autopsy. "Joe *always* had something to say. Joe would've said no," Ransom insisted, if he didn't have anything to say: "That's Joe." (Ransom told me that James had asked that he not be present the night of the execution.) But somehow during the three-and-a-half-hour delay, James had transformed from a devout Muslim and dedicated jailhouse lawyer who, in Ransom's telling, "wanted to fight 'em to the very last minute" into someone mute and absent, with neither an apology for his victim's family nor an utterance of gratitude for their efforts to save his life.

I spoke with Helvetius, Hall's brother, in the days after the autopsy. He told me that he wasn't especially shocked by James's silence, but that he *was* appalled by the state's. In the weeks leading up to the execution, Helvetius said, "Nobody called us, nobody reached out to us, nobody— nobody—got in touch with us." Toni, Faith's youngest daughter, who was a toddler when her mother was killed, told me she had repeatedly asked the district attorney's office to let her speak with James prior to his execution, only to be refused. "There could have been a conversation to heal a little 3-year-old's heart," she said, pausing to swallow tears. But nobody in any position of power, aside from Alabama State Representative Juandalynn Givan, who lobbied the state on behalf of the family, seemed particularly interested in what would bring her or her family peace, much less a sense of closure. They simply wanted James dead.

A CLINICIAN OF 27 YEARS, Joel Zivot worked mainly in intensive-care units and operating rooms before investigating the disappearance of sodium thiopental (an erstwhile anesthetic recruited into lethal-injection cocktails) from the American market circa 2010, due to capital punishment. Zivot's curiosity about the vanishing of a good drug eventually led him to research lethal-injection protocols, at which point he became a vocal critic of the death penalty's use of medical means for lethal ends. Now, having published papers on the bioethical hazards of physician participation in lethal injection and having testified about his research into the suffering evinced by the autopsy reports of executed prisoners, Zivot has become a familiar presence in legal challenges to executions nationwide. Friendships across the anti-capital-punishment advocacy domain made him especially well placed to set up the independent autopsy of Joe James. Within two days of the execution, Zivot had heard rumors about errors, and he began working in earnest to probe the man's death.

Before any exam could take place, James's next of kin would have to agree. I connected Zivot with Ransom to reach out to James's family. "I had my suspicions about the time lapse," Ransom explained, "and I feel like the state needs to be held accountable when they mess up." With that in mind, he called Hakim James, one of Joe Nathan James's brothers, whose mother had charged him with handling his brother's final affairs, and asked if he would agree to submit James's body to an independent autopsy.

Hakim considered, then gave his consent. "I felt it needed to be done," he told me later, even though it came at the end of an already protracted, taxing process. "I felt that it was important."

Then there was the matter of locating an independent pathologist willing to take on the case, and finding the money to pay them. I suggested that Zivot reach out to Reprieve, a nonprofit civil-rights organization made up of lawyers, advocates, and investigators who defend the rights of people facing extreme abuses. Maya Foa, an executive director at Reprieve US, agreed that an independent autopsy ought to happen—quickly.

"Lethal injection was developed to mask the very torture it inflicts," she explained over text message, "and when a prisoner is executed in secret, the only person who can tell the world what really happened is dead. We've seen time and again states suppressing or delaying autopsy results following executions that appear to have gone disastrously wrong. Autopsies help tell the story that the body leaves behind." Reprieve agreed to fund the autopsy through its newly launched Forensic Justice Initiative. By Tuesday morning, Zivot was en route to Alabama from Atlanta and I was making my way from my home in New England; we met in Birmingham, and then went together to the funeral home where the autopsy was to be performed.

The human body opened along "a standard Y-incision"—across the breast and down the center of the abdomen—was unmistakably that of Joe Nathan James. His head was encased in a clear plastic bag, laid to one side, and his face was slack and ashen. The state of Alabama had already wrought its work twice upon James: first in the execution itself, and then again in the autopsy carried out at the Mobile medical examiner's office immediately after, the findings of which would not be made available for a minimum of 90 days, in the optimistic estimation of local capital defenders. And while the array of viscera and the accordion-style slicing of organs was appalling in its bloody gratuitousness—James had been, according to Datnow, a generally healthy man, prior to his execution—it was the story his flesh told about his lengthy and painful death that lent the scene its awful vertigo. In a little green storefront funeral parlor in Birmingham lay the visual record of everything the government can do to you, provided that you, like James in his final hours, have no counsel present, no wealth to your name, and no contact with the outside world.

James, it appeared, had suffered a long death. The state seems to have attempted to insert IV catheters into each of his hands just above the knuckles, resulting in broad smears of violet bruising. Then it looked as though the execution team had tried again, forcing needles into each of his wrists, with the same bleeding beneath the skin and the same indigo mottling around the puncture wounds. On the inside of James's left arm, another puncture site, another pool of deep bruising, and then, a scant distance above, a strange, jagged incision, at James's inner elbow. The laceration met another cut at an obtuse angle. That longer, narrower slice was part of a parallel pair, which matched a fainter, shallower set of parallel cuts. Underneath the mutilated portion of James's arm was what appeared to be yet another puncture—a noticeable crimson pinprick in the center of a radiating blue-green bruise. Other, less clear marks littered his arm as well.

Mark Edgar, a pathologist at the Department of Laboratory Medicine and Pathology at the Mayo Clinic in Jacksonville, Florida, reviewed my photos from James's autopsy and concluded in an email that all of the wounds on James's arm happened before death, judging by the redness along the edges of the wounds. One among them—the deeper, wider cut at James's elbow—suggested, in Edgar's view, "that the inmate moved suddenly while the central cut was being placed, possibly in an attempt to access a vein."

Zivot, upon examining the body, agreed that the incision carved into James's arm was most likely made in the death chamber, in an attempt to expose a vein that execution staff could see. The medical term for the procedure is *cutdown*, and its aftermath dismayed Zivot. "The use of a cutdown in this situation is a stark departure from what would be done in a medical setting," he explained in an email. "I can't tell if local anesthetic was first infused into the skin, as slicing deep into the skin with a sharp surgical blade in an awake person without local anesthesia would be extremely painful. In a medical setting, ultrasound has virtually eliminated the need for a cutdown, and the fact that a cutdown was utilized here is further evidence that the IV team was unqualified for the task in a most dramatic way."

The absence of a local anesthetic during a cutdown, however, could explain two other unusual features of James's execution: the shallow lacerations lining his arm, and the fact that he was evidently unresponsive during the entire lethal-injection procedure witnessed by the media.

Edgar observed that the "roughly parallel" incisions did "not appear to be part of any procedure," but were "more consistent with trauma in my opinion, presumably incurred during a struggle that took place during the pro-longed efforts to gain access to a vein." If James had strug-gled profoundly enough to tear his own flesh with his restraints, that in itself may have prevented IV access. In that case, members of the execution team may have resorted to sedating James.

"I also see several puncture marks not in the anatomi-cal vicinity of a known vein," Zivot wrote in his assess-ment. "It is possible that this just represents gross incompetence, or some, or one, or more of these punc-tures were actually intramuscular injections. An intra-muscular injection in this setting would only be used to deliver a sedating medication."

With roughly one minute elapsing between the read-ing of James's death warrant and the rush of poison into his veins, per witness accounts, it scarcely seems that any-one involved in his execution *expected* him to offer last words. Further, the DOC's own admission that it cannot confirm James's consciousness during the procedure raises an obvious question: Why? James had been alone in DOC custody for the past three hours, presumably undergoing repeated, torturous, abortive efforts to gain lethal access to one of his veins. If something had hap-pened to James during that period that affected his con-sciousness, only DOC staff would know, and the agency's complete failure to account for the last hours of James's life or the awful suffering inflicted upon him before his death is ghastly, the sort of catastrophic, pseudo-medicinal brutality of our recent past that mainly flourishes behind closed doors.

ALABAMA HAD GOOD REASON to think it would never be held to account for what happened to James: He was, at the time of his death, entirely alone, having sought no attendees for his death. In fact, Ransom told me, James had been representing himself in a couple of pending matters before federal courts at the time of his execution, meaning that if he was indeed sedated at some point, what slim semblance of legal counsel he had—his own wits and abilities—was extinguished before his execution.

The thought troubled Ransom. If he had been present, he told me, he would have intervened on James's behalf. There would have been precedent for that kind of intercession: As recently as 2018, Alabama was forced to halt the execution of Doyle Hamm after execution staff punctured his body at least 11 times in his ankles, legs, and groin, apparently even piercing his bladder over a three-hour period. Hamm's attorney, Bernard Harcourt, was there that evening, demanding an explanation for the long delay and preparing a legal offensive for the morning. Hamm's case has since become emblematic of the grotesque reality of lethal injection, compared with its putatively sterile, professional public-facing aesthetics. Lethal injections largely happen, quite literally, behind a curtain;

A

what observers do see looks vaguely surgical; what they don't looks like a war crime.

"The details of the torture inflicted on Joe James are tragic, but unfortunately no surprise to anyone who has had a client executed in Alabama with lethal injection," John Palombi, an assistant federal defender, told me in an email. "Adding to the torture is the refusal of the Alabama Department of Corrections to admit or accurately discuss the issues with Mr. James' execution . . . There should be an immediate moratorium on all executions in the state of Alabama until a thorough investigation of Alabama's execution process, done by people outside the Department of Corrections, is complete."

Megan McCracken, a lawyer based in Philadelphia with expertise in execution methods, told me in an email that, "It is only because of the total lack of transparency surrounding executions in Alabama that the DOC was able to spend such a long time on failed IV access attempts. If this process had been performed openly in front of witnesses, such that anyone outside the DOC knew what was happening at the time, the attempts likely would have been stopped. It is hard to imagine that the courts would countenance this kind of harrowing procedure, but when DOCs can shield their actions and make them invisible to the public, there is no accountability."

Deborah Denno, a law professor and the founding director of the Neuroscience and Law Center at Fordham

Law School, emphasized to me that James's case is only the latest in a long sequence of executions that challenges the constitutionality of lethal injection on Eighth Amendment grounds. "From the very first lethal injection execution to the last—that of Joe Nathan James—the method is predictably disastrous, all the more so in the last dozen years given the lack of availability of drugs," Denno wrote to me in an email. "James's execution not only resembles the execution botches of the 1980s, it is even more egregious given the excessive lack of care and prison officials' indifference to the safeguards of the execution process."

Which is not to say that the state of Alabama will pay any particular heed to this investigation or its aftermath. There is no lobby for dead men. Execution states—24 remain—are, more and more, retreating into secrecy and elaborate privacy laws to hide their execution means and methods. Some states, like Alabama, simply ignore press inquiries into their executions or, as in this case, subject journalists to inexplicable delays and bland, unconvincing evasions. It appears that the state thought no one would catch it at what it was doing, and in most cases it would be correct; that alone is haunting. That it may haunt Faith Hall's family evidently mattered not a jot to the state of Alabama.

The Halls, having fought for James's life, were dismayed and outraged by the news of his torturous death.

In Helvetius's view, he said, Governor Ivey "was wrong for not contacting the victim's family in any fashion, and she was wrong with her statement that Faith Hall got justice. This is not what she would have wanted. And we deserve an apology for that."

Toni Hall agreed, as did State Representative Givan.

The family "simply wanted to be heard," Givan told me. "They wanted an acknowledgment that they were victims and that their voices were listened to and that their concerns were weighed seriously. And I wonder: If they had been white, Anglo-Saxon Americans, would the governor or Attorney General Steve Marshall have at least returned their phone calls?"

Givan reflected that the entire sequence of events had been a grand indignity visited upon a family struggling to heal for more than 25 years, which concluded with the state's utter indifference to their wishes and with James, the object of their attempted mercy, evidently too incapacitated on his deathbed to offer the barest apology.

But there is reason to believe that he intended to.

I spoke with two prisoners on Holman's death row who had known James, spent some of those long years with him, seen him age and change into an older, different man—a committed Muslim who prayed regularly and devoted much of his time to studiously pursuing his own defense, not just for his own purposes, but for the sake of his friends on the row.

One of them told me that James had planned three items for his final words: to apologize to his mother and daughters, to apologize to the Hall family, and to pray the *shahada,* the Muslim profession of faith. He felt grateful for the family's advocacy on his behalf, even startled by it, by the abrupt unilaterality of forgiveness. But he trusted it, and he appreciated it, and he needed it.

James still hadn't chosen the exact words he meant to say, the second prisoner told me. The mind revolts at such closely considered finalities, and James had more reason than most to hope for mercy. Somewhere deep inside, he believed the Halls' forgiveness had saved him.

A

DEAD MAN LIVING

———————

October 2022

AT HOLMAN CORRECTIONAL FACILITY, in Atmore, Alabama, the prisoners have a tradition of beating their doors when guards take a man from the holding area colloquially known as the "death cell" to the execution chamber to be killed. More than 150 men slam their full strength against solid steel, rolling thunder down the halls. It's a show of solidarity with the condemned man— not because he is presumed innocent or absolved, but because the men of death row are uncommonly aware of death's uncompromising egalitarianism. It's coming for all of us, and they mean it when they say it.

Death came for Joe Nathan James Jr. on July 28 of this year, but the lethal-injection procedure that followed the prisoners' last cage-rattling display of camaraderie stretched to roughly three hours, resulting in multiple needle-puncture sites and, eventually, what appears to have been a venous cutdown, or an incision into James's inner arm meant to reveal a vein. (This is not, quite obviously, what is supposed to happen.) Yet in the immediate aftermath of James's execution, John Hamm, the commissioner of the Alabama Department of Corrections, claimed that "nothing out of the ordinary" had taken place in the course of his killing, which might've passed for public knowledge had *The Atlantic* not published the results of an independent autopsy staged shortly after James's death. I was there at the autopsy and saw for myself what they had done to him, all the bruised puncture sites and open wounds. I confess I had hoped the facts of what happened to James might prompt some hesitation among Alabama's legislators about rushing to lethally inject another man. But no Corrections Department representative ever so much as responded to my questions, much less the substance of the reporting: The next execution date kept drawing nearer.

Thus that dreadful clanging boomed through Holman prison again last Thursday, September 22, at roughly 9:25 p.m.—less than half an hour after a lawyer known in death-penalty-litigation circles as "the death clerk" notified Alan Eugene Miller's defense attorneys that the Supreme Court of the United States had rejected Miller's final plea, allowing the state of Alabama to proceed with his scheduled execution. The notification, which soon reached attorneys for the state of Alabama and officials at Holman, began a roughly three-hour countdown to midnight, at which time Miller's death warrant would expire, legally prohibiting the state from any further efforts to execute him until another warrant could be secured—something that takes at least a month's time. The general public was made aware of the Supreme Court's ruling at 9:15 p.m. It came down without any stated reasoning from the Court at all, along with a split: Amy Coney Barrett, a reliable conservative, had voted with Sonia Sotomayor, Elena Kagan, and Ketanji Brown Jackson to stay Miller's execution, pitting the Court's women against the Court's men.

By the end of that surreal odyssey of a night, when Miller was suspended vertically from a cross-shaped table, hands and one foot bleeding in an execution chamber and the state of Alabama apparently realizing it wouldn't be able to kill him within the time it had, Barrett's dissent would seem wise, even prescient. But that would come later. Shortly after we heard the Court's decision, those of us whom Miller had chosen to witness his execution—his sister Cheryl Ellison; brother Jeff Carr; sister-in-law, Sandra Carr; uncle Richard Carr; attorney Mara Klebaner; and me—gathered in front of the Wind Creek casino in Atmore, where the Alabama Department of Corrections elects to rendezvous with witnesses. We passed the time in strained banter until about 10:24 p.m., when a white Alabama Department of Corrections van pulled up in the casino's pick-up lane, and a blue-uniformed guard emerged to direct us inside.

The strip of rainbow neon crowning the casino slumped below the black horizon in the van's rearview mirror. As broad highway narrowed to country road, thick pine woods enclosed us, ringing with cricket and katydid calls. The van passed through gated checkpoints and razor-wire fences, orange floodlights scattering the shadows. The driver and a uniformed corrections officer who rode with him herded us through a guard shack outfitted with a metal detector, then took our phones and identification. A second van drove us a negligible distance up the gated road to the execution chamber.

At 10:30 p.m., two uniformed guards guided us, again, out of the van. This time we found ourselves in a cul-de-sac terminating in the high walls and slit windows of Holman's death row. The squat building sat beside us, its heavy door cracking open, occasionally, startlingly, to spill light into the dimness. But no word came from within. And so we paced, and waited.

Jeff Carr, Miller's brother, wandered alone, contemplative. I walked alongside him after a moment, and looked up into his face to find him chagrined, almost, to have tears in his eyes. All night, Miller's family had carried on this way: good-humoredly, irreverently, and with flinty resolve—but always warm, never forbidding. Neither Alan Miller nor any of his family members have ever disputed that Miller shot and killed three people—Lee Holdbrooks, Christopher Scott Yancy, and Terry Jarvis—during a delusional episode in 1999 that, according to testimony heard at trial, caused Miller to believe the men had been spreading rumors about him. In fact, nobody in

Miller's family present that night registered a general objection to the death penalty—only to torture.

I asked Jeff if he was a praying man. He said he was, and that he'd been doing plenty of that. In the final days of a prisoner's life, the Alabama Department of Corrections permits extended visitation with close relatives and a spiritual adviser, but the rules for their meetings are exacting. A prisoner's family members may share a meal with him but aren't allowed to eat food from the prison's cafeteria or to bring in their own; instead, they're permitted only the soda, candy, and packaged snacks in the on-premises vending machines, a requirement that had forced Alan's younger brother, Richard Miller, and Jeff, each diabetic, to choose between getting sick or losing precious time with Alan to leave prison grounds to eat. They chose high blood sugar and nausea, and stayed with Alan as long as they could.

Standing beside Jeff outside death row, I spent a moment feeling despondent. Since my reporting in August on the last execution that took place on these prison grounds—the botched killing of Joe Nathan James—I have exchanged text messages with several people at Holman, both incarcerated and employed. I often begin my messages with a slash and a circle, like a person waving hello. I looked up and, high inside the prison, saw a man holding a sign: \o.

Earlier that day, I had sent an email to spokespeople for the Corrections Department, asking whether they had changed their execution protocol after James's execution, whether they had trained their staff to establish venous access on a patient of Miller's weight—350 pounds—and whether, in the event they could not, they planned to perform a cutdown in the prisoner's arm, which is not permitted by their protocol, or if they hoped to perform a central-line procedure, which is. I wasn't surprised that they hadn't responded to me; they almost never do. In fact, because all of my efforts to serve as a media witness for the state's last two executions had gone unanswered, I approached Miller with the idea of serving as a personal witness for him. Miller, who was by then well aware of what had happened to James, agreed; Richard Miller lent me his seat among the six spots reserved for Miller's choice of family and friends.

I asked one of the uniformed guards for the time. He told me that it was 10:53 p.m.—and then, calmly, but suddenly, and without any obvious provocation, the two uniformed guards supervising us, who had recently been joined by a Corrections employee wearing a suit and tie, instructed us to climb back into the idling van, which we did, confused and querying. We were told to wait, and we stared through the back windshield at the men as they turned their backs to the van and talked among themselves, gesturing with their arms and rubbing their faces.

A

In about an hour, Miller's death warrant would expire. The blue digital clock on the van's dash was wrong by an odd number of hours and minutes, registering the time somewhere around 9:05. We matched the false hour with the real one given to us by the guard and kept time. It was a hot night, and condensation gathered on the windows as we talked anxiously. Richard worried Alan might be fighting his captors. Sandra Carr, his sister-in-law, worried that he might be hurt. Nobody in their family has good veins, she said. Especially not Alan.

In the distance, more prison vans idled, their headlights hovering on the horizon. Another vehicle passed them with red and blue sirens flashing—*Bizarre,* I thought—and then a stripe of light from the execution chamber opened the night, and we were unloaded into the death chamber shortly before 11:30 p.m.

What followed resembled other executions I have witnessed so much that I was certain Miller was about to die. We were led by wordless guards into a small tiled area focused on an indoor window, which, when unveiled, would provide a one-way view into an execution chamber. The witness room was an oddly proportioned hexagon with cinderblock walls; a glowing rose-pink fluorescent fixture lit three rows of chairs. Signs posted on the walls instructed us to stay seated and be quiet. A blue hospital curtain hung on the other side of the viewing window, in which I could see the reflections of Cheryl Ellison, Miller's sister; Jeff; Richard; and Sandra. Their faces were muted and downcast now, as they waited for the veil to be drawn aside so the state could kill their loved one. Behind us, two uniformed guards stood by the room's only door, and a middle-aged woman in a pantsuit swayed between them serenely, her eyes closed, rocking on her feet as though she were in church.

Mara Klebaner, Miller's lawyer, asked for the time. One of the uniformed guards said that it was 11:35 p.m., meaning that the state had by then had about two and a half hours to set an IV line in Miller, and it still wasn't ready to open the curtain and begin his execution. What on earth had Alabama done to the man?

On the other side of the window, Miller, too, remained under the impression that he was about to die.

Miller later recalled having been strapped down to a gurney at 10:25 p.m. with his arms outstretched, under glaring white tube lights in the same dimensions as his cruciform table. He remembered how the guards took his glasses, and how a trio of men in scrubs appeared and began attempting—unsuccessfully—to establish access to his veins. (Alabama Department of Corrections did not respond to a request for comment on this or other details reported in this story.)

Miller said the men were gentle, and that he asked them casually about the gruesome struggle to set an IV line in Joe Nathan James as they pushed needles into his

A

arms, hands, and a foot. They cut their glances and declined to meet his eyes, he recalled, until one huffed: "Don't believe everything you read."

Over the next 60 to 90 minutes, Miller said, the men stared at, stroked, and punctured his skin in hopes of finding a vein—even producing a pocket flashlight to try to detect a vein visually, and then accepting the offer of a plainclothes corrections officer's cellphone flashlight, but to little avail. Every puncture evidently failed. At one point, Miller remembered the men putting a foam ball in his hand and asking him to squeeze it, which he refused to do. The overhead lights blazed, and personnel moved around the room. Miller couldn't always monitor the clock. Eventually, one of the men began to tap on the veins of Miller's neck.

Miller recoiled sharply. Though the state's protocol permits an execution team to set a central line—a venous catheter often set in the neck or groin—in the event that venous access cannot be established normally, teams had been notably unable or unwilling to successfully set IVs in those locations in other recently botched executions.

At about half past 11, Miller heard a sudden knocking on one of the death chamber's windows. Someone affixed a strap over his chest and jacked the table into a vertical position, and the three men who had pushed needles into him over the past hour-plus departed the room. Miller was left hanging off the upright gurney, his hands and one foot bleeding from failed IV attempts, waiting to die.

After about 20 minutes, he estimates, of Miller asking aloud what was happening to him in the empty silence, an ADOC employee finally answered him, somewhere around five minutes to midnight: "Your execution has been postponed." The gurney collapsed backward, suddenly flat again, and Miller said he saw white light.

If we had known any of this at the time, it may have come as less of a shock when a guard cracked open the door to the witness chamber and said simply: "You may exit."

Miller's family was stunned. "What?" Cheryl asked, staring in disbelief at the man who was now patiently directing us to file out of the prison. They had not yet so much as laid eyes on Miller. How could it be over?

"It's been called off," the man said placidly. We were given to understand that the "it" was the execution, but the circumstances of its cancellation—and the fate of Alan Miller—remained entirely unclear. As uniformed guards rushed us back onto the van, Miller's lawyer and his family demanded to know where Miller was, and whether he was still alive. The guards said they didn't know.

As the van pulled out of the prison grounds, we noticed an ambulance parked adjacent to the execution chamber, which immediately caught the attention of Miller's sister-in-law and his brother, both retired paramedics. They worried something terrible had happened to Miller, and that the authorities had decided to rush him to a local hospital instead of going ahead with the execution—which, in lieu of any other information, made as much sense as anything.

The guards shooed us out of the van and deposited us in the casino parking lot without any further explanation of the night's events; we had no idea whether Miller was dead or alive. While Miller's brother Richard and his uncle, Richard Carr, gathered with other family members waiting at the casino, his lawyer, Sandra, Cheryl, and I rushed to Atmore Community Hospital, the nearest medical facility to the prison. If Miller were the one in the ambulance, we guessed they would take him there.

At 12:31 a.m., I began using my iPhone to film as an ambulance pulled into the hospital lot where we were already waiting, with a white Alabama Corrections Department transport van trailing behind it. But instead of backing into the ambulance bay, the ambulance came to a halt in a hospital parking spot. Klebaner, Miller's lawyer, glanced in the back and was shocked to see that the person inside was not Miller. A single Corrections Department employee emerged from the transport van and said they knew nothing about Miller's whereabouts or condition, but offered to call her supervisor to try to find out. Meanwhile, a paramedic emerged from the ambulance to tell me I wasn't allowed to film. Five minutes later, a caravan of Atmore Police Department SUVs pulled in and a quartet of officers appeared, saying they had been summoned to deal with "a commotion."

Klebaner explained to the officers the rather uncanny situation we found ourselves in: unable to locate a man who was supposed to be dead by now, with no clue as to his condition, or how we might go about finding him. The police admitted to being as baffled as we were.

But I couldn't figure out who had been so troubled by our presence as to call the police, or why. None of us was screaming or shouting, much less behaving aggressively. We were stranded in a hospital parking lot in the middle of the night, soliciting updates from inmates and other attorneys as they came by text message and Twitter. At 12:58 a.m., news finally arrived. Terry Raybon, the warden of Holman prison, pulled into the hospital lot in a white Dodge sedan and parked alongside us, rolling his window down.

Immediately Klebaner asked if Miller was alive.

"Yeah, yeah," Raybon said. "He is in his cell."

At the end of his conversation with Klebaner, Raybon rolled up his window, zipped into a parking spot, took a loud phone call on speaker, and tore back out of the lot. He had promised us a phone call from a Corrections Department lawyer, and within a number of minutes a call did come to Klebaner, though it illuminated little about Miller's whereabouts or condition.

On the other end of the line was Mary-Coleman Mayberry Roberts, the promised attorney, who explained to Klebaner with pleasant briskness that "the execution was simply called off due to the time constraints resulting from the lateness of the court proceedings," a claim similar to what Alabama Corrections Commissioner John Hamm said in a press statement around that time. Roberts repeatedly told Klebaner that "nothing went wrong." Miller was indeed alive and well and in his cell, and that was all she intended to say.

In fact, she seemed annoyed to be on the phone, perhaps displeased by the implication that she or the Corrections Department owed any explanation to Miller's family, who had just spent the past several hours in whiplashing states of hope, horror, disbelief, shock, and suspense. Confronted with such a suggestion by Klebaner, she clarified her purpose. "Ma'am," she said, "we called you as a courtesy because we understood that y'all were at the hospital and worried that that was Mr. Miller. I was calling to let you know it was not, that he is safe, and that's all the information I have to give you at this time."

Klebaner insisted that she be allowed to meet with her client at the earliest opportunity, and pressed Roberts to commit to a time at which they could, at the very least, schedule such a meeting. But Roberts demurred, peevishly, advising her to call during "regular business hours" and schedule an ordinary attorney-client visit. "This is ridiculous and it's not helpful," Roberts finally snapped, hanging up with a curt "Good evening" only a beat later.

Commissioner Hamm would tell reporters that the ambulance that left the prison that night had nothing to do with Miller's execution. The back of the ambulance never opened while we remained, puzzled, in the hospital parking lot, and no further Corrections Department personnel arrived as far as I could see, only the lone driver of the transport van. The only thing I understood confidently by the time we left was that the Alabama Department of Corrections very much wanted us to go.

What do you do the night you were meant to die? Miller would later say that when he was told that his execution had been "postponed," he was unaware that midnight was approaching and still certain he would die, and that when the gurney had been suddenly jolted backward, throwing him into a supine position, his vision had split open to the white light above, and he had believed for half a second he really was dead. But then they had taken the restraints off of him and several guards had helped him to his feet, explaining, finally, that the first ADOC employee had been wrong—that it was after midnight, that the state could no longer touch him, that he had lived.

Miller said that they never returned him to his old cell that night, but rather placed him back in the death cell after a trip to the infirmary, and that the guards brought him a plate of catfish, green beans, and potatoes from the catering spread they'd brought in for the employees working the execution.

At some point after midnight, guards gave Miller a phone and allowed him to call his attorneys and family.

The slot machines were still rolling at 2 a.m. when we crossed back through the casino lobby, numb and wordless under a river of gleaming red and golden feathers suspended and lit from above. We crowded into the hotel room where Miller's brother Richard had placed him on speaker phone, and we listened to the voice of a man who had just survived his own execution.

On Friday, September 23, the day after he was scheduled to die, Miller was permitted an extended visit with his attorney via federal court order, during which time his injuries were photographed. The following day, he was assessed by a physician. That same judge also ordered "personnel employed, contracted by, or otherwise associated with Holman, the Alabama Department of Corrections, and Alabama Attorney General's Office" to immediately preserve all of their communications relating to Miller's attempted execution, "including e-mails, phone calls, text messages, notes, or any other form of communication, written or otherwise." According to Klebaner, "Mr. Miller will continue to vigorously pursue his rights in the ongoing litigation against Commissioner Hamm, Warden Raybon, and Attorney General Marshall, as well as explore all legal options available to him."

Their litigation could help illuminate why the state of Alabama has at least thrice proved itself incapable of executing prisoners via lethal injection in ways that comport with the law, its own protocol, and common sense. Robert Dunham, the executive director of the Death Penalty Information Center, an educational nonprofit organization, told me that Alabama's latest failure to carry out an uncomplicated execution represented an endemic problem.

"This is the third execution in the last five years that Alabama has botched by virtue of their own incompetence in setting IV lines," offering Joe Nathan James and Doyle Hamm, who survived a 2018 lethal injection attempt in the state, as the two prior examples. "Each time, ADOC has denied the obvious and claimed nothing went wrong. They say they've followed their protocol. One of these things must be true: Either they're unreliable, or their protocol is unreliable. Neither one is acceptable when a person's life is on the line." Hamm died of cancer in 2021. Miller thus appears to be America's only living execution survivor.

His family, too, survived something—as did the families of Miller's victims, to whom Governor Kay Ivey

A

extended her prayers early Friday morning, after Miller's execution had been aborted. They most certainly deserve her sympathy, but Miller's family say they haven't heard from the Corrections Department or any other state agency about a debacle that could have, at the very least, been handled with some trace of decency. "Our family was treated like we were guilty by association instead of being there to support a family member in his likely last hours on earth," Sandra wrote to me in an email. On the phone, she told me she felt worn out, like she'd been "rode hard and put up wet," an evocative Southernism for a horse worked up to a sweat under the saddle. I could hear her warm, familiar fortitude, and the exhaustion grinding it down. She is right about what she said—I saw it first-hand, how the prison guards shuffled them from location to location without explanation for cause or delay, and how they were left to wonder for about an hour whether Miller was alive.

Miller's murders were unspeakably wrong—none of his kin dispute that, nor did I ever hear them utter a word to suggest that he ought not be penalized. But neither could I justify, in my review of events, what they had been made to go through that night, at the mock execution of their relative. They were as innocent as anyone, as innocent as you.

Before Doyle Hamm died, he never faced another execution date. Miller may or may not face another night in the execution chamber. If his litigation against the state is successful, it could provide greater detail about a corrections department that appears to be suffering several simultaneous crises, which could, in turn, help other prisoners facing execution in Alabama challenge their own gruesome fate.

The next man doesn't have much time. On Friday, the Alabama Supreme Court declared that in fewer than eight weeks, on November 17, Kenneth Eugene Smith will face his death at the hands of the state. He will presumably die, if Alabama gets its way, in the same chamber that last saw Alan Miller and Joe Nathan James. There is death, there are things worse than death, and, occasionally, there is salvation—and any of them could be in store for Smith.

DEATH OF A SINNER

_____

October 2022

PABLO CASTRO, FATHER OF NINE and convenience-store worker of 14 years in Corpus Christi, Texas, was beaten and stabbed to death for $1.25 on the night of July 14, 2004. His killer was John Henry Ramirez, a 20-year-old ex-Marine who had begun using drugs at 12 and was, by the time he happened to spot Castro taking out the garbage that night, at the tail end of a multiday alcohol, Xanax, and cocaine binge that he was fighting desperately to prolong.

After he murdered Castro, Ramirez fled to Mexico, where he evaded the law for a few years until agents from the Federal Bureau of Investigation captured him near Brownsville, Texas, along the U.S. border. His two female accomplices, who had assisted Ramirez in two other double robberies the same evening Ramirez murdered Castro, were each arrested the night of the killing and sentenced to lengthy prison terms for their roles in the crime spree. The state sought the death penalty in Ramirez's case, and thus began a years-long process of Ramirez countering Texas's efforts to end his life while expressing serious doubts as to whether he deserved to live at all. At his 2008 trial, for instance, after his own father took the stand in his defense, Ramirez asked that his attorneys withdraw all additional mitigation witnesses, further requesting that they read the jury the following verse from Psalm 51:3: "For I acknowledge my transgressions and my sin is ever before me." The jury sentenced him to death unanimously.

In the years that followed, Ramirez's sin was indeed ever before him, recapitulated in court papers and media flares when his legal appeals, at times, succeeded. What he had done had permanently altered a number of lives, his included, and the nature of his sentence painted the balance of his years in shades of guilt and shame. If redemption were available to a man so soundly convicted of his crime, it would have to occur within the confines of his remaining days and without the promise of much ameliorative effect upon his conditions. He would be forced, in other words, to face his sins for honest reasons or to evade them until the bitter end—a dilemma in which few of us would demonstrate much moral courage, and one we spend most of our lives suspending in any case. For Ramirez, there was nowhere to hide.

In 2011, news reports show, Ramirez briefly considered waiving his appeals and hastening his execution. He wrote a letter to Judge Bobby Galvan of Texas's 94th District Court insisting that his remaining legal efforts be suspended so that "justice will be served for the family and friends of Pablo Castro in a speedy fashion . . . they've waited long enough!" In conversations with a prison psychologist, Ramirez said that he would have been willing to carry on with his appeals if he had "support," or "[someone] to show me you care," but that he had neither and, despite his faith in God, he didn't expect any. "I found God a long time ago but I'm not gonna turn holy roller since I ruined my life," he told the psychologist. "God ain't gonna save me."

But before Ramirez could appear for a hearing in Galvan's court, he learned of a paternal half-sister with whom he struck up a relationship, as though the Lord in all his vengeance couldn't resist such a nakedly desperate plea for love. Ramirez reconsidered his desire to end what he had described as his "trash life." His appeals continued until 2017, when his first execution date arrived—"I wouldn't want to ask them to forgive me," Ramirez said of Castro's family at the time. "I just want to ask them to know that I'm sorry"—and passed, thanks to a stay from a federal district court.

Once that litigation was exhausted, Texas set a new execution date for Ramirez, in September 2020. But Ramirez sued in August of that year, arguing that the state's ban on clergy other than staff chaplains employed by the Texas Department of Criminal Justice in the execution chamber violated his religious rights. Specifically, he requested that Pastor Dana Moore of Corpus Christi's

Second Baptist Church, whom Ramirez had met through the pastor's prison ministry in 2017, be permitted to be in the room with him at the time of his death. After some grudging back-and-forth and other delays, the state provided for vetted outside clergy to join prisoners during their execution. But Ramirez, who had found himself transformed by Moore's ministry, gently amended his complaint: He wanted Moore to be able to pray aloud, while touching him.

That turned out to be more than Texas could countenance, and Ramirez's pressing of the matter eventually put his case before the Supreme Court of the United States on the eve of another scheduled execution date, this time in September 2021. Castro's family was distraught, incensed. "Honestly, if he wants a priest to bless him before he's sent off, by all means, go ahead. That doesn't affect me one bit. What affects me is why this process continues to get delayed time and time again," Aaron Castro, one of Pablo's sons, told local media after the Court issued a last-minute stay. "You always think this is going to be the year, this is the time, there won't be another stay of execution, there won't be another delay. He's a disgusting human being . . . Stop crying, stop trying to get around the situation. There's no way out. You need to be executed."

The state of Texas, ineluctable and steady, caught up with Ramirez roughly a year hence, on Wednesday, October 5. Though not without further fight: In April of this year, Nueces County District Attorney Mark Gonzalez filed a motion to withdraw a death warrant another attorney in his office had requested for Ramirez despite the office's policy against such requests, and though Texas privileges the role of local district attorneys in scheduling executions for prisoners, no one seemed especially surprised when the state's courts rebuffed Gonzalez's efforts to save the man. Publicly, it was a shock and an outrage that Texas had rejected a unified attempt on behalf of the prosecution and defense to withdraw the warrant; privately, there was very little likelihood it was going to turn out any other way. And so a little less than two weeks ago, when the state of Texas brought Ramirez into the execution chamber, Moore was there, prepared to deliver the religious rights, and rites, Ramirez had won before the courts.

Ramirez, who lived in certain respects a hard and unforgiving life, took a hard and unforgiving view of himself. He never attested to a dramatic conversion on the inside, just a spiritual transformation that put him back in the mind of following Christ. "There are a lot of people that believe there's a God and just don't live right," Ramirez told a reporter, with respect to his past, in 2021. "I just wasn't obeying, I wasn't trying to be good." Once Ramirez's faith reawakened, he began to rely on Moore's spiritual guidance as his inevitable execution date drew nearer and nearer.

I spoke with Moore last week, after the execution. He sounded drained. He said Ramirez never really forgave himself for Castro's murder. "I'd say about three or four months ago, John was even toying with the idea of not having me in there or anybody on his side, and just let that be all about Pablo Castro's family," Moore told me. "John was genuinely remorseful. It was almost to the point where it was like he didn't want us in there because of penance, and just let it be about their family and just whatever they might need to get peace in their lives," Moore added.

Still, Ramirez reflected in his last moments on his inability to deliver comfort or restitution to Castro's family in any other way. "I just want to say to the family of Pablo Castro, I appreciate everything that y'all did to try and communicate with me through the victim's advocacy program," he offered during his final words. "I tried to reply back, but there is nothing that I could have said or done that would have helped you."

It was as if he were morally inarticulate, but not insensate: Ramirez could hear Castro's family, but couldn't find the right words for them; could feel the love of God, but couldn't always reflect it, either in his dealings with others or in his attitude toward himself.

Moore laid his hand on Ramirez's chest and "prayed [to God] for John to feel his presence, for John to feel his peace, and for everybody there to feel his peace," Moore

A

told me, "because, John first, but it's still everybody else there. It's impacting their lives, and affecting them." John couldn't much react to his prayer, Moore said, which concluded with Psalm 23: "The Lord is my shepherd." Nor did the others in the execution chamber. Moore stood waiting by Ramirez's side, with his hand resting on him, as the man laid before him and died. "I was just praying for God's presence to be with John as he took him home, as he was going to be with Jesus. Just bring that comfort."

Aaron Castro released a statement after Ramirez's death. He quoted Micah 7:18—"Who is a God like you, who pardons sin and forgives the transgression of the remnant of his inheritance? You do not stay angry forever but delight to show mercy"—and hailed a new era of healing for his family: "Peace and Love and justice for Pablo G. Castro, may his name not be forgotten, and may God have mercy in J. H. R. for it is not up to us. He is receiving his true judgment with our Lord and Savior. The Alpha and Omega, the beginning and end. A Life taken away is not to be celebrated but closure can definitely take place."

Micah asks a rational question: What should we make of this peculiar God of this peculiar faith, who rushes to forgive offenses and relieve debts, even if it means sending his emissaries out to where the graver stock of sins are stored, in prisons and penal institutions, even execution chambers? I asked Moore how God saw Ramirez.

"God sees John as he created him," Moore said, not as the sum of all the things he had done. The view of Ramirez from God's eyes, or from Moore's, must seem very strange relative to the assessment the state of Texas made of the man on the day he was sentenced, and held until the night he died. May all our enemies be judged by Texas, and we ourselves by God or Dana Moore.

A

ON MURDERS ESPECIALLY
HEINOUS, ATROCIOUS, OR CRUEL

October 2022

LATELY, IT HAS FELT DIFFICULT to evade the late-'80s countenance of the serial killer Jeffrey Dahmer, an ordinary-looking and affectively blank man with neither the dramatic Jim Morrison locks of his fellow murderer Richard Ramirez nor the sleazy, sinister showmanship of their compatriot Ted Bundy. Rather, Dahmer's recent star turn has emphasized his utter plainness as a kind of counterpoint to his inhuman, almost otherworldly violence—a familiar formula in serial-killer cultural production, in which the criminal's charm, looks, or evident mundanity are balanced against their deeds to provoke a question: What can we make of the fact that such a person could do such things? I suspect that solving this riddle is the honest, if lurid, intention of so many artworks dedicated to Dahmer (and, in different measures, to killers such as Ramirez and Bundy, whose ostensible appeal serves as the counterpoint to their brutality). Acts of such unprecedented, unprovoked destruction cry out for meaning, and the mystique of any given perpetrator handily offers a potential source: Meaning is often hidden inside mysteries, and is perhaps so here.

Yet in so many meditations on these killers and their murders, one never seems to find more than a *recapitulation* of the crimes or life of the criminal, with varying degrees of attention appointed to suggest sites of potential meaning—the serial killer's troubled past, his warped notions of love, his explanation of his own purity of purpose or grandiosity of character. Therein might lie some information that could supply clues about these most spectacular of killings, which would at least situate them in an orderly moral matrix, where things with meaningful effects happen for meaningful reasons. But the *answer* itself—the piece of knowledge that renders the killer or his motives intelligible—never comes. The experience of watching serial-killer shows or documentaries is therefore almost always identical: One now knows more about the grisly nature of what took place, but without the satisfaction of understanding why it had to happen or what to think of a world in which such things occasionally transpire. The viewers—and the victims' families—pay the price for investigating the problem, but they are swindled out of a verdict.

This is because there is no reason, and no meaning, in wanton destruction. It is exactly what it appears to be. It does not entail a greater theory, purpose, or truth of some kind that we could use to our benefit, for prevention or healing, if only we could discover it. It does not respond

A

to the demands of morality or reason, because a moral, reasonable person would not commit acts of vile degradation against other people. What the most spectacular of killers do directly infringes upon the sphere of meaning by eliminating its more common sources in our lives: relationships, plans for the future, love. Dahmer had no reasons, because he was himself a foreigner to reason; what he did had no meaning, but rather, destroyed it. You could climb inside his mind and have no clearer sense than he did of what anything in his miserable life meant, and you would be the worse for it.

Case in point: This year, the state of Florida put Nikolas Cruz on trial in order to sentence him to death for the murder of 17 and the attempted murder of 17 more during his 2018 mass shooting at Marjory Stoneman Douglas High School in Parkland. Cruz had already pleaded guilty, at the time of his sentencing trial, to every count the state had arrayed against him. Everyone knew what he had done. All that was left for a jury to decide was whether, all mitigating factors in the young man's troubled existence accounted for, Cruz's murders were "especially heinous, atrocious, or cruel"—or premeditated with a special disregard for any pretense of justification—according to Florida's capital-punishment statute.

In order to make the case for killing Cruz, the state relied on a meticulous rehashing of the man's crimes, including an in-person tour through the mostly untouched and closed school building where the murders took place, a thorough review of surveillance-camera and cellphone footage of the event itself, and a careful reconstruction of how injured survivors felt at the moment they were assaulted. Somewhere in those accounts or in the autopsy photos or in the witness testimony, the prosecution contended, was proof that Cruz's murders were of a unique and distinct type that would, once revealed through close consideration, necessitate another event, the killing of the killer—and that through that event, some sense of justice would be restored to a community of people who had been radically, catastrophically robbed of such by the murders themselves.

Yet the jury was unable to arrive at a consensus that Cruz should die, with three of the 12 refusing to vote for his death. The reason for the defection appears to be that the prosecution's case did not, in fact, conflict with the defense's in any significant sense. One could believe everything the prosecution said—that Cruz's murders were as unthinkable, as profoundly destructive, as *evil* as they seemed—without disagreeing with the defense's contention that Cruz had done such irrational, unthinkable things because he is, and has been since birth, an irrational, unthinking person. "His brain is broken," Cruz's attorney Melisa McNeill said in her opening statement to the jury. "He's a damaged human being. And that's why these things happen." The defense needed only one juror to realize that that sentiment is entirely compatible with, and in fact credited by, the prosecution's assertion that what Cruz did was "without any pretense of moral or legal justification." Three eventually did.

Their refusal to sentence Cruz to death has already prompted talk of striking jury unanimity, a relatively new requirement in Florida sentencing law, from the state's statute—as though the frustrated momentum of the prosecution's case must find some other outlet. (Had it won, its energy would've likely had to be held in reserve for years, maybe decades, of appeals, as is so common in capital cases.) In the meantime, the trial's participants and witnesses, the general public included, know everything they knew before the lengthy meditation on Cruz's crimes—but worse, more painfully.

We live in spectacularly violent times, not in the sense that our era is more violent than any other before, but rather, that our episodes of especially atrocious violence tend also to become spectacles that play out in the press and culture long after the carnage is over. Part of our fascination is grim curiosity, and part is based, I think, in the sense that some moral work must be left undone, some central mystery left unresolved, if no species of detailed explanation or court action can ever really answer the limitlessness of the void they create in our shared lives. Still, we look into the emptiness. One draws closer and closer, but never comes nearer to anything.

A HISTORY OF VIOLENCE

November 2022

THE CONSTITUTIONAL RIGHT WHOSE protections lie near-est to the skin, flesh, and blood of each American citizen is the Eighth Amendment—the constraint on the govern-ment's ability to punish us in cruel and unusual ways. As with any civil right, if it isn't enforced, it effectively ceases to exist. Because its enforcement ultimately rests with the nation's highest court, it is practically, if not ideally, a matter of politics. And though its disintegration may go unnoticed by those who, through good sense or good for-tune, never encounter governmental punishment, its loss is felt acutely by those who do.

The Eighth Amendment's destruction has now been felt this year by three men subjected to sequential execu-tion proceedings in Alabama—one of whom died, two of whom survived. The state's incompetence at executing its prisoners in accordance with its own protocol has degenerated into a civil-rights crisis, evident in the scat-tered slices and punctures of three executions gone awry in a row.

The latest of Alabama's damned and misbegotten exe-cution efforts unfolded last Thursday evening. I was

A

scheduled to serve as a witness to the judicial killing of Kenneth Smith, a man I had met some months prior, when both of us began to suspect that he would, in all likelihood, soon be the subject of a mangled execution. There was little he could do to stop it, though his attorneys fought tirelessly against dismal odds to avert it, and his family prayed unceasingly for God to save him from what two other men had already endured.

What providence did hold for Smith was a severe and bracing mercy: After two days of back-and-forth among three of the nation's courts concerning his Eighth Amendment rights and the potential of his impending execution to violate them, Smith was strapped down to a gurney for hours and tortured until his executioners simply gave up on killing him.

The Monday after Alabama attempted to kill Kenneth Smith, Governor Kay Ivey released a statement announcing a de facto moratorium on executions until "the Department of Corrections undertake[s] a top-to-bottom review of the state's execution process" so that "the state can successfully deliver justice going forward." In the view of the governor's office, the ordered investigation, to be carried out by the very agency responsible for three consecutive disasters, is a regrettable but necessary step to guarantee that victims' families are no longer promised executions the state cannot deliver. "For the sake of the victims and their families, we've got to get this right," Ivey said in her press statement. That the Alabama Department of Corrections has repeatedly jeopardized, if not outright violated, the constitutional rights of some of her state's own people seemed not to weigh heavily on her mind.

In 1988, Smith, then a 22-year-old father of four children, confessed to taking a murder-for-hire job from a 21-year-old friend of his named Billy Gray Williams, who had earlier been contracted for the murder by Charles Sennett, a pastor. The target of the plot was Sennett's wife, 45-year-old Elizabeth Sennett, whom he wanted killed in a mock robbery gone wrong so he could collect an insurance payment. Smith was joined by another friend, John Parker, in the scheme. Sennett was to pay both men $1,000 for their participation in his wife's murder, on top of whatever they felt like stealing while ransacking the house.

When he admitted to the crime, Smith said that he had been an active participant in planning the hit and carrying out the robbery—a Samsung VCR stolen from Sennett's home and discovered in Smith's possession proved crucial in establishing his guilt—but denied that he himself had beaten or stabbed the pastor's wife. Those acts he attributed to Parker, who, along with Smith and Williams, was promptly brought to trial on charges of capital murder.

The jurors considering the fates of Smith, Parker, and Williams had an immediate problem to confront: The mastermind of the plot to murder Elizabeth Sennett, the *if not for* cause of the slaying, was Charles Sennett—and he was, by the time of the legal proceedings, already dead by his own hand. He had committed suicide within one week of his wife's murder, as soon as the investigation began to close in on him, orphaning their children and leaving prosecutors with the trio of men he had enlisted to perpetrate his crime.

Not all criminal sentencing is strictly about making the convicted person pay. Courts can order therapy or rehabilitation or other forms of pro-social and restorative programs built around reform and reintegration, with goals that surpass the merely punitive. But in capital sentencing, the entire premise and point is making the convicted person pay. The sentencing portion of a capital trial finds the law at its most theatrical, with prosecutors dramatizing the brutality, forethought, cruelty, and malice that seal men's fates, and the defense providing by way of mitigation everything that provokes mercy in a soul: details of the defendant's childhood, invariably terrible; an exploration of the man's cognitive and emotional limits, in most cases considerable; a portrait gallery of loved ones and friends to frame a picture of a person who deserves to live. *Whether* the convicted person will be punished is not in question, only *how,* and it is the prosecution's task to argue that the balance of justice cannot be restored unless he pays the ultimate price.

When the ringleader of a particularly heinous crime is already dead at the outset of a trial, the criminal-justice system cannot right the scales of justice. By the purported logic of the death penalty, the suicide of a culpable perpetrator ought to be proper enough restitution for the original homicide—the ultimate price is death, and the right person has paid it. But the emotional logic of crime and punishment requires not that someone *pay* but that someone be *made to pay*; not just that someone dies but that someone is killed. For Smith, Parker, and Williams, Sennett's suicide was in that sense especially inopportune. They were the only ones left to be made to pay the ultimate price for Elizabeth Sennett's murder.

For his role in the murder, a jury sentenced Billy Gray Williams to life without parole. By a vote of 10 to 2, another Alabama jury sentenced John Parker to life without parole as well—but his trial judge nullified that decision and sentenced Parker to death nonetheless, an old-fashioned outrage known as "judicial override." Parker was executed in 2010.

Kenneth Smith was sentenced to death in 1989, but his sentence was overturned on appeal in 1992. Upon resentencing, a jury gave him life without parole by a vote of 11 to 1. A judge promptly overrode their decision, sentencing Smith to death again in 1996. In 2017 Alabama became the last state to ban the practice of judicial override, but the prohibition didn't apply retroactively: Smith's death sentence held.

Now, five years later, he was scheduled to die. If the state had learned from its acknowledged mistakes, it would have selected for its next execution a man whose sentencing didn't come about through what is now understood to be a miscarriage of justice. Then again, if the state were in the habit of learning from its mistakes, it wouldn't have sent anyone into its death chamber at all.

This past summer I picked up a call from Joel Zivot, a physician at Emory University Hospital and an expert on lethal injection. That call led me to Birmingham, Alabama. There, I observed the autopsy of Joe Nathan James Jr., a man killed by the Alabama Department of Corrections on July 28. James's execution had been observably unusual per contemporaneous local media reports: It was delayed by three hours, and then it proceeded without many of the mainstays of judicial killings, including the apparent consciousness of the condemned or any last words.

Alabama was never able to confirm to media that James was conscious at the time of his execution, nor did it supply a convincing account of what had transpired during the long pause prior to James's lethal injection. To protect executioners' identity, their work occurs behind drawn curtains, unseen by attorneys for the condemned or by the press. Witnesses see only a man strapped down to a cross-shaped gurney, two catheters inserted into two veins, typically one in each arm. If the executioners succeed in laying those catheters and thus preparing the man for his death, then the only detailed account of what took place behind the curtains is their own.

An ADOC spokesperson said in an email to the media only that the execution team had struggled with "intravenous access" in James's case and added that it has the right, per its own execution protocol, to set a central line—an intravenous catheter usually inserted in the neck, chest, or groin—if the team is incapable of establishing standard IV access. But, it said, that hadn't happened.

What *had* happened is a story told by James's body, which has become the subject of fierce legal debate. The body I saw that early-August afternoon in Birmingham had clearly been pierced several times by needles on the hands and arms, suggesting a process of trial and error. More troubling were a series of cuts on the left inner arm, near the elbow. Some were shallow and long; one was deep and short, perhaps cut with more conviction. None of them was explicable per ADOC's execution protocol, which mentions nothing about whatever ghastly and bungled procedure this was—likely an attempted "cutdown" in search of a visible vein. (Alabama has denied performing a cutdown on James and has neglected to offer any

A

other explanation of what happened to the man's body in their custody.)

ADOC has since insisted that nothing particularly out of the ordinary occurred during James's execution. Yet Alabama's own Department of Forensic Sciences recently released an autopsy report that lists, under the subheading "Evidence of Injury," the very cuts on his arm that, per protocol, had no business being there. James's autopsy also found that the executioners had pierced his foot as well, echoing the attempted execution of Doyle Hamm, a man Alabama tried and failed to kill in 2018. After looking over the state's autopsy report and my photographs of James's body, James Gill, Connecticut's chief medical examiner and a pathology professor at the Yale School of Medicine, told me in an email that "there are recent, parallel incised wounds (cuts) of the left forearm and antecubital fossa (crux of the elbow). The deepest one is next to a puncture site of the antecubital fossa (the crux of your elbow) . . . Directly under this area are the large veins of the arm . . . the antecubital wound is consistent with an attempt at a 'cut-down' to gain access to a vein."

To date, nobody, including the state of Alabama, has produced a clear explanation for how the cuts on James's arm got there, or who made them. In the absence of an alternative theory, a parsimonious guess would implicate the executioners. The inexpert and haphazard nature of the work was, for legal challenges that later cited James's case, precisely the point. This wasn't the meticulously plotted and diabolically perfected torture of a sadist, but the effortful failure of someone who was trying to achieve something somewhat beyond them. As a sinner looking over their endeavors, I identified; as a citizen, I was horrified.

The next execution effort did little to improve my impression. On September 22, ADOC attempted to execute Alan Miller, a man I met shortly after publishing my story about what had happened to James. My requests to serve as a media witness at recent executions had gone unanswered, so Miller asked me to serve as a personal witness, and I readily agreed, convinced that the authors of James's execution were unlikely to pull off a flawless killing eight weeks later. With their identities still cloaked in secrecy, the executioners pierced Miller's hands, arms, and foot with needles for somewhere around an hour, searching for veins under his skin with the aid of a cellphone flashlight and blindingly white fluorescent lights overhead before considering a site to puncture on his neck—when a tap came from the other side of an observation window, signaling that the execution had been called off. Someone (this person's identity remains unknown) had evidently decided that the executioners were unlikely to succeed in getting a needle into Miller's neck just moments before midnight, when his death warrant would expire. Miller, unlike James, had a lawyer present on prison grounds.

A

Miller's attorneys were quick to chase his attempted execution with a series of complaints, one of which persuaded R. Austin Huffaker Jr., a federal judge in Alabama's Middle District, to rule on November 15—two days before Kenneth Smith's scheduled execution—that the Alabama Department of Corrections had to provide the names of its executioners to Miller's attorneys one week hence. If the executioners could be known, then they could be deposed, and their answers under oath could shed some light on why Miller's attempted execution had transpired the way it did.

And James's execution, for that matter. This point—that the secrecy of the entire execution procedure, from personnel to practice, renders it nigh impossible to know what exactly keeps going wrong behind the curtain in Alabama's executions—haunted the end of oral arguments in Smith's appeal before the Eleventh Circuit. That hearing took place a mere 28 hours before Smith was to be executed. Almost no one knows who the executioners are, or why they can't seem to kill people without inflicting needless suffering, or how they could be meaningfully sanctioned without being revealed in some way. A panel of three judges on the Eleventh Circuit took the evening before Smith's scheduled execution to deliberate. The Supreme Court denied a separate petition that night.

Holman Correctional Facility is hidden among the dense marsh forests of lower Alabama, which are nourished by the Escambia River and its tributaries, among the many alluvial waterways that snake toward the Gulf of Mexico as the South fades into the ocean. After nightfall, the prison grounds can be forbiddingly dark, but not on the night Smith was to die.

Instead, Holman was lit by stadium-style floodlights brought in by corrections officials, creating an unusual and dramatic setting for what the state had sworn in court would be a by-the-book execution. Likewise, ADOC brought in patrol teams with canines to police the facility's perimeter for the duration of the event, as though the greatest risk to seamless executions in Alabama weren't already inside the death chamber, contemplating their tools.

I arrived at the Wind Creek casino, operated by the Poarch Band of Creek Indians, which happens to be the nearest accommodation to the prison, before dusk and joined Robert Grass, one of Smith's attorneys, all of whom were in the midst of managing their client's last appeals. Capital defense attorneys, a wry and ironical breed, refer to the final legal maneuvers prior to a client's execution as "end-stage capital litigation," a clinically precise term for a chaotic period in which time both shrinks and dilates, and cases that have idled in courts for years rocket through hearings and rulings at warp speed. Inevitably, a sense of momentum begins to build. As the writer Janet Malcolm once observed, legal papers written in one's favor are among the most affirming and optimistic documents a person is likely to read in a lifetime, and one could be forgiven, as such papers are passed up to the highest courts of the land, for believing in their promise.

There is time inside that hope, and it spreads open into an intense, immediate present. Smith's mother, sister, sons, daughter-in-law, and wife, Dee, gathered at another nearby hotel, keeping in close contact with me via cellphone. Although the state liaises with the families of the victims in a capital case, no such provisions are made for the perpetrator's family, whose only offense is being related to the offender. They're left alone to patch together news from media reports and the sporadic updates of understandably preoccupied defense attorneys. It is a tense and nerve-racking process that the state makes worse through its resolute indifference, as though the torture of a prisoner's family were part and parcel of a proper execution. Loved ones wait, and do as they are told. Any text, tweet, or telephone call could mean news of life or death. Adrenaline rises early and remains high.

In those hours, reversals can arrive suddenly. As Grass and I waited in a hotel room, Smith was denied a stay in district court. Smith's attorneys immediately appealed to the Eleventh Circuit, which had ruled in his favor earlier that day and sent the case back to the district court. At 7:44, despite the fact that Smith's appeal was pending, the state notified Smith's attorneys that it was "preparing

Mr. Smith for execution," meaning—as far as we could tell—that it intended to begin attempting access to Smith's veins, though the poison, we assumed, would not flow until the courts had made their final rulings. Somewhere near 8 o'clock, guards removed Smith from his cell and transported him to the execution chamber, where he was strapped down to the gurney.

I knew what to expect next: a phone call from the secretary of the warden of Holman, who would tell me and Grass to head to the front of the casino, where we would be picked up in an ADOC van and taken to prison grounds, walked through a metal detector, marched into a witness room, and shown an execution. I called Dee about the district court's denial of Smith's stay, to make sure she was informed and to ask if she was ready for the next steps. She was straining to maintain her composure against the worsening circumstances. She had been visiting frequently with Smith for the past several days, during the extended visitation hours permitted the week of a prisoner's execution, and communicating with him via telephone for the past several hours. But then their communication had abruptly stopped. And the next call to come would be—

—a stay from the Eleventh Circuit, which, when announced to Dee and Smith's mother and children on the other end of the line, elicited shouts and clapping and

A

cries of joy; *he could make it now,* it seemed, as the clock ticked closer to midnight, and the expiration of Smith's death warrant. In the hotel room with Grass, emotions were subtler: Though Smith had prevailed in the Eleventh Circuit by convincing the judges that, based on Alabama's recent history, his lethal injection would present an unconstitutional risk to his Eighth Amendment rights, I strongly suspected that once the case reached the Supreme Court later that night, the six conservative justices would not be so moved. The Court has never in its history outlawed a method of execution. Indeed, in recent years it has issued rulings in Eighth Amendment capital-punishment cases that have raised the bar for receiving mercy progressively higher.

A little before 10:20 that night, the Court vacated Smith's stay without explanation. (The Court's three liberal justices dissented.) Now, again, we waited in silence for the call from the prison that would lead us outside to wait for the van that would transport us to Smith's end. Now, again, all the despair and despondency came. Every trilling slot machine and dinging elevator bell echoed through the casino walls as we waited for the telephone to ring. We said nothing.

Time passed. The boxy digital clock on the hotel nightstand flashed 10:30, 10:36, 10:45. I wondered if the prison had deliberately neglected to contact us. Dee hadn't heard anything either; she just waited, shattered. Eleven o'clock arrived. I looked at Grass and realized that Alabama was botching another execution.

BY THAT TIME, Smith told Dee and me in a phone call later that night, he had been strapped to a gurney in Holman's execution chamber for more than three hours, since 8 o'clock, after his request for a stay had been denied in district court. Although Alabama's executioners didn't begin trying to access his veins then, neither did anyone from Holman or the state of Alabama bother to tell Smith about the stay that the Eleventh Circuit instated some time after the district court's decision—he simply remained strapped to the gurney intended to be his death-bed, bound and uncertain, as the evening sloped toward midnight. The executioners turned their attention to him only after 10 o'clock, when the Supreme Court vacated the stay, extending them its written invitation.

At that point, Smith recalled, three men entered the chamber and busily set about forcing needles into his flesh, to place their catheters. They were successful once, Smith said, in his left arm. And then, evoking the ordeals of James and Miller, site by site, the men began to fail: piercing Smith's right hand once, twice, three times; working the needle in and tugging it out, trying a different angle two, three, four times; then moving on to his feet, surveying there, having no success; then switching to

A

his right arm to repeat the process begun on his left. When Smith's other veins were spent, one of the men moved toward his neck.

Now, Smith told us, one of the executioners donned a clear face mask and threw a surgical covering with a transparent plastic opening over Smith. He asked Smith to turn his head. Smith refused, and a deputy warden from another correctional facility clasped his head and twisted it to the side. Then the executioner pushed a large-gauge surgical needle into Smith's chest, just beneath his collarbone, searching blindly for his subclavian vein to establish a central line.

Smith could feel the needle stabbing him "like a knife," and he protested the pain, which the executioners insisted he should not be able to feel, because they had already injected an anesthetic. Whatever they had given him, it did little for the pain and nothing to get them closer to a vein.

"And I kept telling them," Smith told Dee and me, "call the fucking judge. My case number is 2:22-CV-497. Somebody in this fucking room call the judge or call my lawyer." (Nobody at ADOC responded to a request for comment about the events of that evening.)

But nobody said a word. Not to Smith, when he was objecting to the acts that would later form the substance of his reinstated legal complaint against the state of Alabama, and not to Smith's family or his attorneys when state officials decided, sometime around 11:20 p.m., that there was no more point in trying to access Smith's veins before midnight. Instead, we surmised that Smith had survived his execution from reporters gathered at Holman to serve as press witnesses, who began tweeting that they were being removed from idling prison vans outside the execution chamber and taken back inside the media center.

At midnight, when Smith's death warrant finally expired, Governor Kay Ivey published a statement expressing her regrets that the state had been unable to kill Smith and her confidence that "attempting it was the right thing to do." She offered her prayers to Elizabeth Sennett's children and grandchildren, who, she said, were being "forced to relive their tragic loss," though she neglected to specify by whom.

The state of Alabama seemed to contend that Smith had foiled his own execution through cynical last-minute legal trickery, at the expense of honest justice. But every prisoner on death row is entitled to such end-stage legal appeals, and every capital defense attorney goes into the hours before an execution prepared to protect their client's interests to the best of their abilities. None of that was unusual, nor did the time constraints imposed by the legal proceedings actually represent a significant barrier to getting a needle into a second vein: Lateness of the hour aside, executioners still pierced and injected Smith for more than an hour, and called off their efforts with more than 30 minutes left on the clock.

What happened to Smith appears quite similar to what seems to have happened to Joe Nathan James, and what certainly did happen to Alan Miller: For reasons that remain unclear due to the anonymity of the executioners and the secrecy surrounding their qualifications, training, and activities inside the death chamber, the IV team tasked with accessing Smith's veins once again failed after many attempts. Its efforts this time did not include a cutdown, but culminated with their protocol's most extreme contingency, a central-line procedure. Such an outcome was what Smith's own final appeals had predicted; the prisoner himself proved a more accurate assessor of the Alabama Department of Corrections' capacities than the agency and its lawyers. Then again, the people subject to the capital-punishment regimes of execution states have more cause than anyone to carefully study their captors.

Smith, like Miller, is litigating his botched, aborted execution. He is also recovering from a surreal and terrifying experience that, whatever one makes of it, was not part of his sentence, and indicates both Alabama's stunning incapacity to perform executions that comport with the Constitution and the state's bold indifference to any requirement to do so. There is no official involved with Alabama's capital-punishment edifice who does not realize that the state's executions and executioners have a serious problem.

Alabama's failures in the execution chamber are extreme, but not unique. The week Kenneth Smith was to be killed, three other men were executed via lethal injection in the United States: Stephen Barbee, in Texas; Richard Fairchild, in Oklahoma; and Murray Hooper, in Arizona. The IV team in Hooper's case struggled with venous access and wound up inserting a catheter into his femoral artery; likewise, in Barbee's case, executioners failed to properly insert needles into the man's veins for half an hour before setting a central line in his neck.

One can blame the right of the condemned to defend themselves in this nation's courts, or one can blame them for their unwillingness to die. But the most proximate cause of America's cruel-and-unusual-punishment problem is the fact that this country still countenances judicial killings, which, while carried out in the name of the American people, dissolve our rights little by little.

ALABAMA MAKES PLANS TO GAS ITS PRISONERS

December 2022

CRITICS CALLED 2022 "the year of the botched execution"—and it was indeed an infamous period, mainly because the state of Alabama lost the ability to competently kill prisoners in its charge while retaining the sovereignty to try.

On July 28, Alabama executed Joe Nathan James Jr., a convicted murderer. And, for some reason—the precise cause remains a mystery because of the extreme degree of confidentiality the state guarantees its executioners—the execution team working that night botched their task badly, piercing James all over his body before evidently cutting into his arm, presumably in search of a visible vein in which to insert an IV catheter. They nevertheless managed to kill him, the results of their work clear in the early-August autopsy I witnessed. I left that experience convinced that Alabama's next execution would also likely unfold against protocol.

With that in mind, I headed to Alabama again on September 22, the scheduled execution date of another man, Alan Eugene Miller. I was there that night when, after an hour or more of failed attempts, executioners exhausted their efforts at getting two needles into two of Miller's veins, and state authorities called off his death.

Undaunted by its two consecutive failures in the execution chamber, Alabama promptly scheduled another death-row prisoner, Kenneth Smith, to die. I immediately made Smith's acquaintance and agreed to attend his killing as well. On November 17, Alabama again tried and again failed to execute its man. Smith spoke with me later that night, once he was back in his cell, and told me how his would-be executioners had pierced his arms and hands and finally his neck underneath his collarbone before abandoning their efforts.

At that point, Alabama finally acknowledged what had been clear to me since early August: Inside the state's execution chamber, there is a crisis deserving of investigative review. On November 21, Governor Kay Ivey ordered a temporary halt to executions so that the Alabama Department of Corrections could assess its execution methodology and personnel before moving forward. But this is not to say that Alabama is evolving; if notions of progress were distributed evenly among the states, this would be the point in the story where I would be able to report that this series of botched executions had caused Alabama's leaders to consider abandoning the death penalty altogether. Instead, Alabama is choosing a path of technical, rather than moral, innovation.

The state appears to be preparing to premiere a new kind of execution by lethal gas. In the gas chambers of old, little cells were filled with poison that eventually destroyed the organs of the trapped prisoners, resulting in death. Now Alabama proposes to use nitrogen gas to replace enough oxygen to kill via hypoxia, an untested method once imagined in a *National Review* article and made manifest in a plastic gas mask.

Chief Justice Earl Warren made a certain presumption about the relationship between moral and technological progress, and that presumption shaped his interpretation of the Eighth Amendment, which bans cruel and unusual punishment. It went like this: As societies develop, their moral sensibilities tend to become more refined as well. Or, as Warren put it, writing in *Trop v. Dulles*, "The Amendment must draw its meaning from the evolving standards of decency that mark the progress of a maturing society." In other words, Americans ought to aspire to more and more humane means of punishment, and the law ought to be understood as cooperative in that effort.

And yet, though several methods of execution have fallen into disfavor across history, the Supreme Court has never formally *banned* one, instead allowing states to choose from many archaic ways to kill prisoners. Lethal gas, for example, remains an artifact of the past and a specter of the future, both lethal injection's inferior predecessor and its current statutory alternative in a small number of states—Alabama among them.

America's executions with gas began roughly 100 years ago, at the outset of a century that would witness the industrial-level use of cyanide in Germany's death camps. Scott Christianson's book *The Last Gasp: The Rise and Fall of the American Gas Chamber* notes an inflection point in America's experiment with gas in March of 1921, when Nevada Governor Emmet Boyle signed the Humane Execution Bill into law, requiring future executions to be carried out with lethal gas. The new law endeavored to replace older, uglier methods—hanging and electrocution—with a manner of dying that was promised to be painless and bloodless. Instead, on February 8, 1924, Nevada prison officials led the Chinese immigrant Gee Jon to a converted stone barber house that would be flooded with a gaseous form of hydrocyanic acid commercially known as cyanogen, a highly toxic substance used industrially to manufacture fertilizer and exterminate insects. Witnesses watched through the brick outbuilding's window that morning as Gee gasped and convulsed amid the haze of lethal gas that filled the chamber. One military physician who observed the execution that day would later report that the death house's heating had failed, causing the gas to partially liquefy rather than vaporize, then collect on the floor of the chamber where it remained in a deadly pool for hours after Gee's death. That same physician would also later speculate that Gee, who had been poisoned on a frigid day at roughly 9:45 a.m. and who was not removed from his shackles until after noon, had likely died of cold and exposure.

Nevertheless, the execution was hailed as a coup for progress: Finally, after all of the bodies twisting on nooses and smoking under electrocution hoods, there was a scientific, humane execution method. Around the world, people took note: In Soviet Russia, Leon Trotsky was certain that America would soon turn its dastardly weapons on revolutionary Europe; in Germany, the news was met with great interest by researchers for the cyanide industry and budding fascists alike.

More than 600 people have died in American gas chambers since Nevada's 1924 experiment. Remarkably, states used gas to execute prisoners even after the term *gas chamber* became synonymous with Nazi Germany. Though the chamber had promised instantaneous and painless death, the ugliness and risk of its application eventually made it the country's shortest-lived method of execution, Deborah Denno, a professor at Fordham University School of Law, told me. In plain view of witnesses, prisoners died screaming, convulsing, groaning, and coughing, their hands clawing at their restraints and their eyes bulging and their skin turning cyanic.

The last of them, Walter LaGrand, was killed in Arizona in 1999. Despite the length of time separating his death from Gee's, he endured a similarly troubled execution: LaGrand, a German-born American who was convicted of murder, gagged and hacked and then died over the course of 18 minutes. Knowing what prison authorities intended to do well before they strapped LaGrand into the black harness that would contain his body as he choked on poison gas, the government of then–German Chancellor Gerhard Schröder had tried diplomatic interventions to save the man's life. The irony was lost on Arizona.

Alabama has something slightly different in mind. Nitrogen hypoxia is the dream of Stuart Creque, a technology consultant and filmmaker who, in 1995, proposed the method in an article for *National Review,* in which he speculated optimistically about the ease and comfort of gas-induced death. After hearing about the potential of nitrogen hypoxia as a lethal agent in a BBC documentary, Oklahoma State Representative Mike Christian brought the idea before Oklahoma's legislature in 2014 as an alternative to lethal injection. Oklahoma passed a law permitting the use of nitrogen hypoxia as a backup method of execution in the event that lethal injections could no longer be carried out. Mississippi passed similar legislation in 2017; Alabama followed in 2018. With Missouri, California, Wyoming, and Arizona (which have older lethal-gas statutes still on the books), these three nitrogen-curious newcomers make up the handful of governments that could begin attempting to execute people with lethal gas at any time. (The Alabama Department of Corrections did not immediately reply to a request to comment for this article.)

Alabama is by no means the ablest of these states, but it is among the more eager. Since the governor announced an execution moratorium pending an investigation, Alabama's attorney general, Steve Marshall, has been adamant that the killings will resume as soon as possible. "Let's be clear," Marshall recently said at a press conference he called to dispense his thoughts on the subject. "This needs to be expedited and done quickly, because we have victims' families right now asking when we will be able to set that next date and I need to give them answers," adding that "justice delayed is justice denied."

Court papers provide clues about where Marshall's insistence upon speedy executions translates into an interest in gas. Earlier this year, Marshall's deputy attorney general, James Houts, brandished a gas mask during the deposition of Alan Eugene Miller, one of the men the state tried and failed to execute via lethal injection this fall, and asked Miller if he would be cooperative if prison officials attempted to fit the mask to his face or if he would be upset by the process. A witness to the event described the mask as a large plastic covering that would obscure most of the face, and which was to be locked in place by wide lime-green straps arrayed around the mask like the fixtures of a headlamp. Houts all but assured Miller's attorneys and a district-court judge that Alabama would be prepared to execute Miller on September 22 of this year via nitrogen hypoxia, though he could not say directly and unequivocally that the state had actually finished developing its nitrogen-hypoxia execution protocol.

Unsurprisingly, Alabama officials weren't ready, and thus they attempted to kill Miller this fall with the usual cocktail of lethal drugs piped in via needle. Still, their presentation with the gas mask during Miller's proceedings demonstrated something useful about their approach: Unlike the gas houses of yesteryear, the state is evidently preparing to use a sealed mask attached to some source of nitrogen gas in order to induce hypoxia in a restrained prisoner. For this method of execution to kill successfully, the state will need access to the mask and its tubing, nitrogen gas or its precursors, a sealed chamber for the safety of bystanders, and a detailed plan.

Nitrogen is cheap and widely available, but also extremely dangerous. It has been used as a method of suicide and has killed people in industrial accidents. Deployed at a prison, it could pose a risk to staff in the event of leaks. Just last year, a liquid-nitrogen leak at a Georgia poultry facility resulted in six deaths and 11 hospitalizations. The Alabama Department of Corrections is aware of these risks: James Houts admitted during a court hearing in November that "the fact that there's nitrogen gas stored in a certain place" presented "the dangers of inert-gas asphyxiation to employees."

Houts added that the state had attempted to contract with a Tennessee-based firm to diagnose and improve its gas-execution system. But that firm terminated its contract with the state in February of this year after protests from local religious leaders, leaving the ADOC without an obvious alternative. This month, a spokesperson for Airgas, a national industrial-gas distributor that has done business with the ADOC in the past, told me over email that "notwithstanding the philosophical and intellectual debate of the death penalty itself, supplying nitrogen for the purpose of human execution is not consistent with our company values. Therefore, Airgas has not and will not supply Alabama nitrogen or other inert gasses to induce hypoxia for the purpose of human execution." Airgas's spokesperson added that the company's contact in Alabama had been notified of this position upon my outreach. Few vendors, it appears, want to be directly involved in America's return to the gas chamber.

Alabama will need a finished protocol taking all of the above into account before it is ready to execute the first American by nitrogen hypoxia. As of this fall, state officials seemed not to have one. It would take a certain audacity to be the first state to test an unknown means of execution immediately following three consecutive botched executions. But Alabama's administrators are nothing if not audacious.

A

ARTICLE CREDITS

A

ABOUT THE AUTHOR

ELIZABETH BRUENIG is a writer at *The Atlantic,* where she arrived after stints at the *New York Times* and the *Washington Post.* She is a two-time Pulitzer Prize finalist for feature writing, most recently in 2023 for her work in *The Atlantic* on death row inmates in Alabama. Liz reports on capital punishment, criminal justice, and American violence. She lives in Connecticut with her husband and two daughters and two cats.